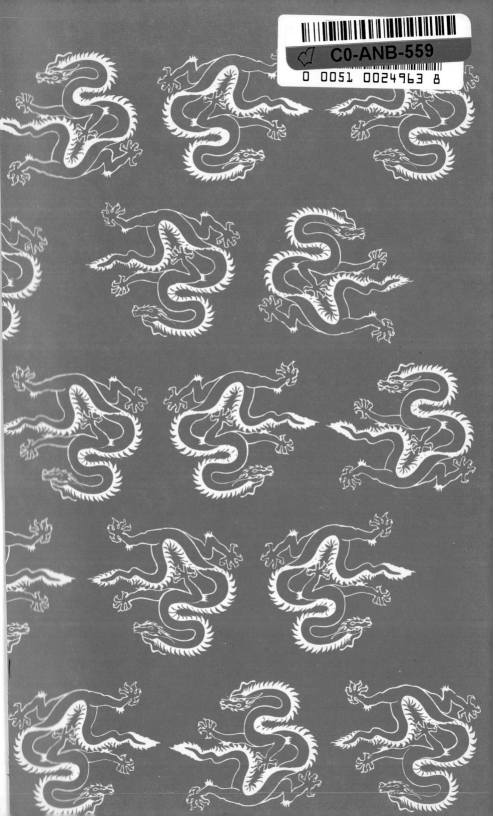

ORIENTAL IDEAS IN RECENT RELIGIOUS THOUGHT

by
O'Hyun Park

Published by CSA Press
Lakemont, Ga. 30552

Library of Congress Catalog Number 73-83915

Standard Book Number 0-87707-129-2

Printed for the publisher in the United States of
America by CSA Printing and Bindery, Inc.

CONTENTS

INTRODUCTION

For some time now oriental religious ideas have been entering the consciousness of occidental men, and there has been increasing interest in them both by laymen and scholars. A vast scholarship has arisen as texts have been translated and commented on. The influence of the orient is discernible in modern art, poetry and psychiatry as well as in popular culture and anti-culture.

Interpreters of oriental religious ideas frequently have seen them as historically or otherwise conditioned, and many even set aside the inwardness of oriental religions as one of those mysteries about which nothing can be said. Of course, it is the responsibility of scholars to concern themselves with philosophy, ethics, sociology, anthropology, psychology, and aesthetics, and to analyze religion from these and other perspectives. Oriental religious traditions do have ethical, sociological, philosophical, anthropological, and psychological conditions and consequences, but may they not also express a reality which escapes through the meshes of a purely objective or causal analysis?

In other words, suppose there is a central core to oriental spirituality to which most occidental students, and not a few modern oriental students give insufficient recognition? Would they not in that case fall short of the deepest understanding of the essential intention of oriental religions? It is the possibility of such an inmost centrality which this dissertation undertakes to explore as well as the extent to which the inattentiveness to it has limited the evaluations of oriental religious ideas by such eminent thinkers as William Ernest Hocking, F.S.C. Northrop, Hajime Nakamura, Fung Yu-lan, Bhagavan Das, Allan Watts, Albert Schweitzer, Aldous Huxley, S. Radhakrishnan, Winston L. King, Henri de Lubac, Thomas J. J. Altizer, Martin Buber and others who will be subjected to scrutiny in this dissertation.

No particular religion is herein advocated or set up as archetypal whether Hindu, Buddhist, Confucian, or Taoist. Although this study is concerned with these four oriental religious traditions, its approach is neither like Schopenhauer's which took Indian religions as normative nor like Hegel's which took Christianity as the highest. Instead, it wishes to transcend religious differences, in order to try to get at the commonality of oriental religious consciousness.

The claim that there may be a common thread running through the major religions of East Asia may not seem to have *prima facie* plausibility. The diversities seem far more numerous and far more important than the resemblances. And this will continue to seem the case for anyone who is unwilling to depart from the purely factual approach to the materials.

The proper alternative to external and objective analysis is not a relapse into sheer subjectivity but the adoption of an integral approach to the religious quest of the orient which sees it as a human quest. Human life is ever a mysterious conjoint of the subjective and the objective, and its deeper significance is never yielded to anyone who approaches it as an objectivity alone. Human truth is to be apprehended only when approached in ways that are fully human and that demand of the investigator that he bring to the task all that he is, not solely an isolated intellect which can objectify all that it grasps and rejects all that it cannot objectify. As one may study the formal structure of a poem or its historical antecedents and yet be totally unresponsive to its poetry, so objective researches into human spirituality do not fully reveal its spirit. But it is the spirit which gives life without which there is only the corpse. It is the deepest perspective of this dissertation that oriental religions are not simply collections of thoughts or disciplines. They express an inner intention which is—as we hope to make clear—to appropriate, i.e., to make one's *own*—the source of life or the living truth.

Logically viewed, the standpoint of the dissertation is at least paradoxical. It has set itself to show by the methods of modern scholarship that there is possibly a substantive depth in oriental spirituality which is not attainable by "critical scholarship." The most one can hope to achieve in this way is to interest the world of scholarship in the further exploration of the possibility as well as in the possible limitations of so-called "critical scholarship" in the area of religion. Our procedure is simply to elucidate the possibility, to give it *some* documentation (a conclusive validation by scholarly documentation being ruled out by the very nature of the possibility) and to evaluate some recent interpretations of oriental thought in the light of this possibility. The reader is asked to remember that the official stance of the dissertation is the examination of a possibility which has far-reaching ramifications; if at times the language seems to suggest a more dogmatic affirmation this is only because the writer has temporarily been carried away by his deeper "biases" in the area. That this discussion of the possibility may lead someone to reexamine his own approach to the religious culture of the orient is for the writer a sufficient justification for the undertaking.

We are therefore not operating under the naive presumption that we have presented the actual essence of oriental spirituality. The living substance of oriental religious culture may be likened to a mountaintop. This dissertation has not undertaken to reproduce the view from the mountaintop. It has only attempted to point to the mountain which needs to be climbed by anyone wishing to enjoy the view, and to call the wayfarer's attention to paths which lead in other directions.

We have worked with a sampling of contemporary religious thought. It is only a sample. Like all samples, it is limited. It is defensible as a sampling on the grounds of being broad, variegated, multi-national and multi-religious and therefore, hopefully, representative of certain tendencies in the interpretation of oriental religious thought. The thinkers selected have not only made a substantial effort to grasp the essence of oriental spirituality, but also in most cases their philosophical orientation has the humanistic breath and existential awareness to support their efforts. The sample would seem to warrant the conclusion that there may not be a widespread awareness of the central thrust of oriental religiosity and that this lack may be related to long engrained patterns of dualistic thought.

These same patterns of thought particularly characterize the methodology of those who choose to limit themselves to objective, external and purely intellectual treatments of religions as packages of doctrines and practices which have been historically conditioned, and who refuse to confront them as living realities, to meet them on their own grounds and to understand them in their own terms. They would grasp them as objectified commodities and view them from the perspective of the external spectator rather than from the perspective of the living participant. Such an approach is often based on the metaphysical bias that reality is sheer objectivity and hence the more objective a study the closer it will be to reality. But the "bias" of the orient is that reality is encountered in wholeness, that what excludes subjectivity can never be wholeness, and that the dualism of subjective-objective must be broken through before the living truth may be known.

This study has not been conceived as a proof and defense of the oriental bias in this matter. Its purpose has only been to clarify the intent of oriental culture and to show that at least a large number of influential evaluations of it misconstrue its intent and operate from premises which it does not share.

It can be said that many of those who clamor most loudly for a critical methodology seem to be uncritical in regard to their own critical methodology. That is to say they seem unconscious of the unproven assumption on which this criticality rests. That reality is pure objectivity, that it will open itself to purely intellectual analyses, that religions are simply historically or otherwise conditioned and have no truth base or ontological grounding—these are some of the undemonstrated presuppositions of much "critical religious scholarship." They are not self-evident axioms and they are not universally accepted.

The orient, as we shall see, does not share them, and it may not be ruled out of court for that reason. All that needs to be said at this point is that if critical scholarship is right, then the orient has been pursuing a fantasy. If the orient is right, then critical scholarship is doomed to an increasingly devitalized irrelevance. The question of which one is right is not to be decided by the arbitrary and pontifical proclamation of a simple methodology as alone suitable for serious students. Methodology does not dictate the nature of reality. Methodology if it is to disclose reality must be adapted to the nature of reality, otherwise it becomes tyrannical and procrustean. An axe is a useful tool in relation to wood. It will not enable one to shave but that is merely a limitation of the axe. It does not prove that hair does not exist or that it cannot be dealt with by another instrument. If a man limits himself to the axe as his only instrument, that is his prerogative, but it is a decision about what he will do, not about the nature of things as such. Scholars who limit themselves to a preconceived method to study reality do not thereby determine the nature of reality. They are only limiting their own exposure to reality.

The choice of method is never determinative of reality but only of the form of reality which the user of the method allows himself to confront. The fundamental question then is whether studies of religions should be limited to studies of the formal dimensions of religion, or should they also involve effort to confront the realities of religion? The forms of a religion can be studied or known externally and objectively. But reality can only be known by reality. And to enter into the reality of a religion, one must also enter into one's own reality. Of course one cannot simply ignore objective data. This has its own validity and the objective is an ingredient of the whole. But it is only an ingredient and in the end one must confront the large mystery of the relation of the objective and the subjective. Integral scholarship cannot limit itself to either the intellectual or the existential alone, but must see them in their creative non-duality. Otherwise scholarship remains in the deplorable condition described in the following:

> I recall a monk in Hong Kong who had copied an important manuscript, which he allowed me to photograph. I suppose that I made quite a fuss over it, since it seemed to be the only copy extant. He himself was impressed neither by the manuscript nor my enthusiasm for it. He kept urging me to join his group for a year's intensive meditation in a makeshift meditation hall. Shortly after my departure he wrote a letter to say: "You should not go to Treasure Mountain and then come home empty-handed." My suitcases were full of material on Chinese Buddhism, but I know what he meant.[1]

Historically, questions of methodology have often become central at times when there has been a loss of contact with substance. In other words, the less there is to talk about, the greater the worry about "how to say it." While methodological considerations are important, they are not all-important. Many scholars of religion today have labored over methodology, even as they have emptied their discussions of religious substance, and much objective scholarship may

[1]Holmes Welch, *The Buddhist Revival in China* (Cambridge: Harvard University Press, 1968), p. 268. And the full statement was: "You should not go to Treasure Mountain and then come home empty-handed. You must bring back a little nourishing, absolute dharma (*we-sheng fa*) to Harvard University. What is this dharma of the absolute? It can make you happy in body and mind, lengthen your life, eliminate all illness, and only through it can your research colleagues at Harvard obtain release by getting the sweet dew that you may bring them." In the same chapter (*op. cit.*), p. 354.

be motivated by the wish to evade the confrontation with religious reality or by premature despair of finding it.

We are not, needless to say, arguing against methodology as such any more than we should want to argue against the careful pursuit of knowledge. We are in fact asking for an enlarged and more flexible methodology which would not limit itself to one side of the subject-object dichotomy alone. Every methodology finally presupposes an epistemology, and every epistemology presupposes a metaphysic [and behind every metaphysic is the living individual]. We would only insist that neither methodolgy nor epistemology can determine what is finally real. Their proper task is only to determine what is involved in the act of knowing the real and in what ways the gathering of knowledge may be most fruitfully effected. A study of religion which aims to fearlessly face religious reality must shape its method to its task. It cannot simply mimic objective methodologies in science or history. An integral methodology for the study of religion is inseparable from the question of man's own reality and it cannot be based on the duality of seeker and sought or of subject and object or of substance and method. Bellah has recognized this crucial point:

> . . . if we believe what we have long said in the tradition of the study of religion out of which I come, namely that religion is concerned with the deepest dimensions of human experience, with the problem of man's wholeness, how can we keep those issues out of the classroom without hopelessly distorting the very subject we are attempting to teach? Personally I am not afraid, as I said in the last chapter of my recent book, of blurring the boundary line between religion and the teaching of religion. Above all we cannot accept as eternal the way that boundary has been drawn in the past. Indeed the whole issue of boundaries and separations in the academic world is involved in the present crisis. We have gone such a long way in specialization and differentiation that our whole culture is threatening to come apart at the seams. It is certainly a time to think in new ways about integration, about how things might fit together in new ways. We need not lose all the benefits of the old

differentiation if we realize that diffcrentiation and integration are dialectically involved with cach other and require a kind of rhythmic alternation of emphasis for healthy growth. One of the special opportunities in teaching religion at the present is that it is one of the few fields concerned with integration, with problems of the whole. Perhaps it is the only such field now that philosophy at so many universities is given over to narrow technicism.[1]

Religion, which is concerned with the problem of the whole, requires the wholeness of the researcher. It will not reveal its totality when it is approached with partiality. Methodology has to be ontologically related to its object. The ontological meeting of method and substance is for the oriental perspective no other than man's true selfhood. For the orient,

Being is not to be grasped speculatively but is only to be entered into existentially. One knows reality to the extent that one is real, and the problem is not to formulate an objective and formal criterion of reality, but to be real oneself . . . the question . . . is not: 'What is Being qua Being?' but 'How do I contact my own true being?'[2]

And again to quote Bellah:

. . . let me say that teaching religion in a way that tries to respond to the current cultural crisis is itself a kind of religious discipline. For how can one try to integrate culture if one does not also try to integrate oneself? Norman O. Brown said recently in talking about his own development that he had been trained to be an abstract intellectual, and an abstract intellectual is a mind without a body. I realize that when I started teaching I was a disembodied ghost presenting abstract concepts. I have finally learned that that really isn't teaching. Especially in the present situation students are not going to care about the little generalizations

---

[1]Robert N. Bellah, "Confessions of a Former Establishment Fundamentalist" in *Council on the Study of Religion* (Hanover: The American Academy of Religion, 1970), Vol. 1, No. 3, December, pp. 5-6.

[2]Bernard Phillips, "Reflection on Zen and Humanism" in *The Humanist,* Vol. xxviii, No. 6, November and December, 1968, p. 16.

you give them for purely abstract reasons. They need to see humanly why there are important. I have learned that the primary resource you have as a teacher is yourself, your whole self, mind and spirit and body, and unless you are willing to teach with your whole self, with everything you have, you are not really going to teach at all. Needless to say, I haven't gotten very far in my efforts. But I can say that every effort has been enormously rewarded.[1]

To this the orient will say "Amen." It would add that what is true of the teacher is also true of the student, and to paraphrase Bellah, the primary resource you have as a student is yourself, your whole self, mind and spirit and body and unless you are willing to study with your whole self, with everything you have, you are not really going to study at all. To penetrate oriental religious culture, all the student must be brought to bear on all that this culture is, and the more complete the non-duality of student and subject-matter, the greater is the depth and the deeper the truth of his grasp of it.

In short, the inwardness of oriental spirituality is not to be acquired by hermeneutical virtuosity and the scrupulous decoding of texts alone but by the holistic encounter with it as a living thing and with living representatives and teachers. Oriental religion has always transmitted itself not primarily through the written word but through the personal mode of religious apprenticeship. Texts are in the end externalizations, formalizations, codifications of something more intimately living which the text at its best can point to but not directly convey. Finally the seeker for religious reality must go beyond texts to find "that before which all words recoil."

Hopefully, therefore, this study may be of threefold value: first, it may serve as something of an antidote to a good deal of contemporary scholarship, insofar as it clarifies the extent to which interpretations of oriental religious traditions are conditioned by provincial patterns of

[1]Bellah, "Confessions of a former Establishment Fundamentalist," p. 6.

thought and arbitrarily limited methodologies. It is typical of occidentals as well as of many contemporary orientals to wish to study religions by means of merely objective understandings of religious ideas. These objective studies of world religions fail to transmit their living essence, and in consequence, those whose approach is purely of this sort may conclude that God is dead and religion is not necessary to human life.

Among the differences between traditional oriental thought and contemporary objective religious scholarship is this one: Oriental religious thought is existentially oriented in the sense that its aim is to direct man to the full possession of his manhood. Hence, if it is true, it is not just pointing to a truth, but to the pearl of great price. Objective scholarship has no such intention. If it is true, it is simply factually true, and still leaves man with his spiritual needs unsatisfied. Man's spiritual thirst will not be quenched at the fountain of objective learning, and if that is all there is, then he would be doomed to remain thirsty. In that case, we should be left with the mystery: How comes it that the human species is endowed with this thirst which nothing in this world or out of it can quench?

Second, it is our hope that this study may contribute to religious anthropology, insofar as it may broaden the perspective of discussion of the human religious situation by directing *anthropos* to the question, "Who am I?" To the orient, this question is not merely anthropological or psychological but fundamentally religious. All other serious questions of human existence involve this question. Without an answer to "Who am I?" all answers to other questions are suspended in mid-air, simply because the questioner himself remains questionable. Kant's questions, "What can I know?" "What ought I to do?" "What may I hope?" are to the orient abstract and thus dead questions. These questions are put objectively and seek objective answers and thus do not confront the "I" who puts the question. The ultimate and fundamental question—that is, "Who am I?"—will not be answered at the dualistic level where question and questioner are separated and the question is merely considered intellectually. In contemporary thought, anthropology, theology, philosophy, ontology, psychology, and ethics are pursued separately. For the orient, they are spokes of one wheel whose hub is the true self. Without the hub, the spokes have no point of unity and the wheel must crumble.

And last, this study aspires to contribute to comparative religious thought, insofar as it hopes to clarify the underlying unity as well as the diversity of oriental religious traditions. Each oriental religion expressed a particular tradition, and yet goes beyond it. Though rooted in different historical backgrounds and experiences, oriental religions show an underlying unity of thought in the continuing endeavor to find the ultimate truth of life which is not separable from the ultimate truth of self. *Brahman, atman, tat tvam asi, nirvana, buddhahood, sunyata, tao, wu-wei,* or *jen*—it is the underlying claim of this dissertation that all these point to one reality: the non-duality of subject and object.

I am not aware of any other attempt at a synoptic review of oriental religious influence from the standpoint of non-duality. Chapter I provides partial documentary support of the hypothesis through a discussion of some key texts drawn from the four major religious traditions of East Asia: Hinduism, Buddhism, Confucianism, Taoism. Chapter II presents a number of contemporary appraisals of oriental religious culture as a whole and evaluates them in the light of our hypothesis. The following three chapters focus respectively on Hinduism, Buddhism and Confucianism-Taoism as seen through the eyes of some eminent contemporary religious thinkers.

CHAPTER I

NON-DUALITY IN ORIENTAL RELIGIOUS CULTURE

Many attempts have been made to formulate the distinction between oriental religious culture and occidental religious culture. The great religions which arose in the Fertile Crescent are said to be religions of history, not of nature; they are monotheistic holding to a personal God rather than to an impersonal absolute; and they often distinguish sharply between the creature and the transcendent creator; they are rooted in a revelation by this creator of his nature and wishes, and man's task is to conform to these wishes, etc., etc.

This dissertation undertakes to examine a more fundamental dimension of the religious contrast between East and West, and to differentiate the fundamentally non-dualistic approach of the orient from the fundamentally dualistic orientation of occidental man.

The latter is taken as a premise and not as a probandum. We assume it as a valid characterization of traditional occidental religious culture that it grasps the world as dichotomized or polarized between subject and object, matter and spirit, ultimate and immediate, good and evil, here and hereafter, nature and history, self and others, creator and creature, reality and appearance, essence and existence, etc., etc.

Occidental religious thought has endeavored to cope with these dichotomies and in general reveals three tenden-

17

cies: one gives primacy to the categories clustering about the pole of immediacy of reality. This is the tendency variously called naturalism, materialism, secularism, etc. A second gives primacy to the categories clustering about the pole of transcendence. This has appeared under such names as idealism, transcendentalism, supernaturalism, etc. A third affirms the middle-of-the-road position of dualism, to wit, that both are equally fundamental. The main currents of religious thought all flow in one or another of these directions.

Religion for occidental man has generally meant a pledge of allegiance to the pole of transcendence in human life as against a life centered in the immediacy of here-now. It is the pagan or the hedonist or the naturalist who has succumbed to the satanic lure of immediacy, but the religious man lives by a law and for a goal which are not wholly of this world. In the final analysis, neither of the opposing renditions of significance of human existence has really achieved the peace that passeth understanding, for each secretly longs for what the other possesses and is completed by it. Therefore St. Paul's cry, "Wretched man that I am! Who will deliver me from this body of death?" where the "members" war with the law of the spirit. And hence also Faust's "Zwei Seelen wohnen, ach, in meiner Brust." Where the world is dichotomized man is also dichotomized. And the dualism which would mediate the opposites by proclaiming the necessity of both simply states the problem; it is not itself the solution.

Is there a solution within the framework posed by the problem? Or must the framework be thrown out and, with it, the problem? In other words can it be that the problem admits of no solution in its own terms, but only of a dissolution?

If so, the real problem is the dichotomy itself, that is the grasping of life as something intrinsically fissured. And the real solution would not come from perpetuating the dichotomy by an opting either for one pole or the other or for a middle position, but from relating to life in a way that is non-dichotomous to begin with and which poses no such problem from the start.

Such—if we have grasped its deeper meaning—has been the approach of the orient. As expressed in the four major Far Eastern religious traditions—Hinduism, Buddhism, Confucianism, and Taoism, it has involved the search for a life which is not plagued by duality and in which there is no need to choose between opposites. It is the common search for that which will give wholeness and the common conviction that it is not to be obtained by exclusion on the plane of opposition which justifies the use of the phrase *oriental religious culture* as more than a geographical appellation. Of course, from the standpoint of critical scholarship we may seem to be begging a question. No doubt we can point to the quest for the life of non-duality as an ingredient in the above-named religious cultures and as embodied in some of their representatives. But how do we establish that it is the highest aim of the culture and its ultimate essence? This is not finally to be established by documentation. In setting forth any version of any culture, the subjectivity of the interpreter comes in as an ingredient. Which passages speak to him, which exemplars he takes to be exemplary, which works and which periods, represent heights and which depths—not all of this can be objectively established.

It is the hypothesis underlying this dissertation as well as the bias of its writer that the quest for a non-dualistic life is the key to the deepest intentions of oriental religious culture and that its neglect leads to distorted appraisals of that culture. As explained above, the purpose of this dissertation is not primarily to fully authenticate that bias, but rather to illumine its meaning, to show that it is directly pointed to in many texts, and to argue that it is worth further consideration as possibly illuminative of oriental religious experience as a whole. The defense of the hypothesis in full detail is probably beyond the capacities of anyone living today, since it would require (a) an intimate knowledge of at least five or six oriental languages and their reli-

gious literatures, (b) a firsthand acquaintance with the
socio-religious life of the cultures using these languages, (c)
a firsthand acquaintance with teachings and disciplines of
the oral traditions of these cultures which is obtainable
only through discipleship.

It is by virtue of his full awareness of his own limitations that the writer puts forward his hypothesis as a "gut
intuition" based on his own experience as an oriental and
his broad but still necessarily limited readings in the major
oriental traditions. At this point he is only prepared to assert that there are some documentary grounds for asserting
the possibility to be a very real one. Let us proceed to a
brief examination of some of the better known articulations
of the non-dualistic approach in the four great traditions of
East Asia.

In the earliest sacred literature of Hinduism, the search
for the ground of being is formulated as an ultimate question:

> Who knows this truth? Who can explain it? From what
> does this multiformed world come forth? Who created it?
> Even the gods are created after the first creation. Then
> how can they know about the first creation before them?
> Then how can any one know it?
>
> Who knows from whom the world comes out or whether
> he forms it or does not form it? He who resides in the
> highest heaven perhaps knows it. Or does he also not
> know it?[1]

The *Upanishads* are wholly centered on the quest for
the ground which they name *brahman* when it is regarded
as transcending the individual. *Brahman* cannot be identified objectively. As Yajnavalkya, the great teacher of the
Brihadaranyaka Upanishad puts it:

> Now, therefore, the description of Brahman: 'Not this,

[1]*Rgveda*, 10: 129, as compiled by P. T. Raju, "Religions of India," *The Great Asian Religions*, compiled Wing-tsit Chan, Isma'il Ragi al Faruqi, Joseph M. Kitagawa, and P. T. Raju (London: The Macmillan Company, 1969), p. 21.

not this'; for there is no other and more appropriate description than this 'Not this.' Now the designation of Brahman: 'The truth of truth.'[1]

The same is called *atman,* when it is viewed as the inmost reality of the individual. The teacher goes on to say that:

> This self is That which has been described as *Not this, not this.* It is imperceptible, for It is not perceived; undecaying, for It never decays; unattached, for It is never attached; unfettered, for It never feels pain and never suffers injury.[2]

Its immanent aspect, *atman,* and its transcendent aspect, *brahman,* are ultimately not two. As the *Isa Upanishad* puts it:

> It moves and moves not; It is far and likewise near. It is inside all this and It is outside all this.[3]

The ultimate search is for something which cannot be objectified and yet which supports all that is objective. Nor is it merely subjective though it is at the heart of all subjectivity. It is both prior to and beyond the duality of the subjective and objective. A Brahmin's son, Svetaketu asks his father about the truth of truths. His father replies:

> (The father said) "Bring me a fruit of that nyāgrodha (banyan) tree."
> "Here it is, venerable Sir."
> "Break it."
> "It is broken, venerable Sir."
> "What do you see there?"
> "These seeds, exceedingly small, venerable Sir."
> "Break one of these, my son."
> "It is broken, venerable Sir."

[1]*Brihadaranyaka Upanishad,* II. iii. 6., as translated in Swami Nikhilananda, *The Upanishads* (New York: Harper & Row, Publishers, 1964), p. 200.

[2]*Ibid.,* III. ix. 26., p. 237.

[3]*Isa Upanishad,* 5., as translated *ibid.,* p. 90.

"What do you see there?"

"Nothing at all, venerable Sir."

(The father said:) "That subtle essence, my dear, which you do not perceive there—from that very essence this great nyāgrodha arises. Believe me, my dear."

"Now, that which is the subtle essence—in it all that exists has its self. That is the True. That is the Self. That thou art, Svetaketu."

It is the One "before whom words recoil." No language can convey its essence.

It is not possessed through knowledge nor can we authentically relate to it in ignorance and knowledge. As the *Isa Upanishad* paradoxically expresses it:

Those who worship ignorance (avidyā) enter blinding darkness; those who worship knowledge (vidyā) enter a thicker darkness.[1]

The *Mundaka Upanishad* points to the "higher knowledge" which transcends both ignorance and knowledge:

. . . The lower knowledge is the Rig-Veda, the Yajur-Veda, the Sama-Veda, the Atharva-Veda, siksha (phonetics), kalpa (rituals), Vyakaranam (grammar), nirukta (etymology), chhandas (metre), and jyotis (astronomy); and the Higher Knowledge is that by which the Imperishable Brahman is attained.

By means of the Higher Knowledge the wise behold everywhere Brahman, which otherwise cannot be seen or seized, which has no root or attributes, no eyes or ears, no hands, or feet; which is eternal and omnipresent, all-pervading and extremely subtle; which is imperishable and the source of all beings.[2]

. . . By the knowledge of That which shines as the bliss-

---

[1] *Chhandogya Upanishad*, VI. xii., as translated *ibid.*, p. 334.

[2] *Mundaka Upanishad*, I. i. 5-6, as translated by Nikhilananda, *loc. cit.*, p. 109.

ful and immortal Atman, the wise behold Him fully in all things.

The fetters of the heart are broken, all doubts are resolved, and all works cease to bear fruit, when He is beheld who is both high and low.[1]

The difference between the higher knowledge which breaks the fetters of the heart and the knowledge of objects which does not have this transforming power is not a difference of degree but of kind. The higher knowledge, unlike the ordinary knowledge, is not analyzable into relation between known and knower:

> . . . Brahman as the eternal subject (*pratayagātman*, the inward Self) is never an object, and . . . the distinction of objects known, knowers, act of knowledge, etc. . . . is fictitiously created by Nescience.[2]

From the highest standpoint of oriental spirituality, nescience is the duality or unrelatedness of knower and known, and it functions to distort or mask reality:

> A man may, in the dark, mistake a piece of rope lying on the ground for a snake, and run away from it, frightened and trembling; thereon another man may tell him, "Do not be afraid, it is only a rope, not a snake"; and he may then dismiss the fear caused by the imagined snake, and stop running. But all the while the presence and subsequent absence of his erroneous notion, as to the rope being a snake, make no difference whatever in the rope itself. Exactly analogous is the case of the highest soul, although Nescience makes it appear different.
>
> As therefore the individual soul and the highest Self differ in name only, it being a settled matter that perfect knowledge has for its object the absolute oneness of the two; it is senseless to insist (as some do) on a plurality of Selfs, and to maintain that the individual soul is different from the highest Self, and the highest Self from the individ-

---

[1] *Mundaka Upanishad,* II. ii. 8, *ibid.,* p. 114-115.

[2] Sankara, "Brahman," as quoted from John A. Mourant, *Readings in the Philosophy of Religion* (New York: Thomas Y. Crowell Company, 1956), p. 87.

ual soul. For the Self is indeed called by many different names, but it is one only.

The Self is thus the operative cause, because there is no other ruling principle, and the material cause because there is no other substance from which the world could originate.[1]

And to regain reality—to attain the "realization" which is the goal of Hinduism—the duality must disappear. Shankara says:

Liberation cannot be achieved except by the perception of the identity of the individual spirit with the universal Spirit. It can be achieved neither by Yoga (physical training), nor by Sankhya (speculative philosophy), nor by the practice of religious ceremonies, nor by mere learning. . . .[2]

The Truth cannot be grasped externally or objectively:

He who knows the Supreme Brahman verily becomes Brahman.[3]

'I tell you this, the secret Brahman (essence): there is nothing greater and more important than man.'[4]

The non-duality or relatedness of seeker and sought is also expressed by Sri Ramana Maharshi in the following way:

Since the Self cannot be objectified, not being cognized by anything else, and since the Self is the Seer seeing all else, the subject-object relation and the apparent subjectivity of

---

[1]Ibid., p. 89.

[2]Quoted in Aldous Huxley, The Perennial Philosophy (New York: The World Publishing Company, 1968), p. 6.

[3]Mundaka Upanishad, III. ii. 9, as translated in Nikhilananda, loc. cit., p. 118.

[4]Mahabharta, as quoted from P. T. Raju, "Comparative Philosophy and Spiritual Values," in Philosophy East and West (October, 1963), p. 225.

the Self exist only on the plane of relativity and vanish in the Absolute.

There is in truth no other than the Self, which is neither the seer nor the seen, and is not involved as subject or object.[1]

Because the individual self, which is nothing but the mind, has lost the knowledge of its identity with the real Self, and has enmeshed itself in bondage, its search for the Self, its own eternal primal nature, resembles that of the shepherd searching for a lamb which all the time he bears on his own shoulders.[2]

Knowing one's own Self is knowing God. Not knowing the nature of him who meditates but meditating on God as foreign to one's own Self is like measuring one's shadow with one's foot. You go on measuring while the shadow also goes on receding further and further.[3]

Buddhism is no less resistant to a purely objective analysis than is Hinduism. It is wholly foreign to its central intention to view it as a set of ideas that may be examined by an impartial spectator. Buddhist spirituality begins with the Buddha's enlightenment, that is with Buddha's actual realization of the non-duality. It can be said that this enlightenment was not metaphysical but existential. The existential quality of the experience is plain in the following:

Long have I wandered! Long!
Bound by the chain of desire
Through many births,
Seeking thus long in vain,
Whence comes this restlessness in man?
Whence his egotism, his anguish?
And hard to bear is samsara
When pain and death encompass us.

---

[1]Arthur Osborne, ed., *The Collected Works of Ramana Maharshi* (London: Rider & Company, 1959), p. 25.

[2]*Ibid.*, p. 30.
[3]*Ibid.*, p. 36.

> Found! It is found!
> The cause of selfhood, (Author of selfhood,)
> No longer shalt thou build a house for me.
> Broken are the beams of sin;
> The ridge-pole of care is shattered,
> Into Nirvana my mind has passed,
> The end of cravings has been reached at last.[1]

And as a teacher, the Buddha functioned as a physician, not as a metaphysician. The Buddha himself describes more vividly the human existential situation in the following words:

> And what, Māluṅkyāputta, have I elucidated? Misery, Māluṅkyāputta, have I elucidated; the origin of misery have I elucidated; the cessation of misery have I elucidated; and the path leading to the cessation of misery have I elucidated. And why, Māluṅkyāputta, have I elucidated this? Because, Māluṅkyāputta, this does profit, has to do with the fundamentals of religion, and tends to aversion, absence of passion, cessation, quiescence, knowledge, supreme wisdom, and Nirvana. . . .[2]

He dealt with man's existential predicament. He was not concerned with appeasing the mind's insatiable appetite for ideas. Human existence is prior to reason. It is existentially true to say that man exists, therefore he thinks. Reason being an aspect of life can never encompass the full reality of life; reason can grasp only what it can objectify. But what is living eludes objectification and thus defies rational analysis:

> Those who vainly reason without understanding the truth are lost in the jungle of the Vijnanas (the various forms of relative knowledge), running about here and there and trying to justify their view of ego-substance.

[1]Paul Carus, *The Gospel of Buddha* (Chicago: Open Court Publishers, 1914), p. 33.

[2]H. C. Warren, *Buddhism in Translations* (New York: Atheneum, 1963), p. 122.

The self realized in your inmost consciousness appears in its purity; this is the Tathagata-garbha (literally, Buddha-womb), which is not the realm of those given over to mere reasoning. . . .

Pure in its own nature and free from the category of finite and infinite, Univeral Mind is the undefiled Buddha-womb, which is wrongly apprehended by sentient beings.[1]

The unreasoned truth cannot be taught by any man. The truth, which Buddhism points to, is existential in the sense that it cannot be objectified without falsification. It cannot be grasped by the intellect alone but only with one's whole being. One must become the truth to know it. In no other way can it be known:

The truth indeed has never been preached by the Buddha, seeing that one has to realize it within onseself.[2]

What is known as the teaching of the Buddha is not the teaching of the Buddha.[3]

"What is the ultimate teaching of Buddhism?" "You won't understand it until you have it."[4]

With the lamp of word and discrimination one must go beyond word and discrimination and enter upon the path of realization.[5]

The Tathagatas do not teach a Dharma that is dependent upon letters. Anyone who teaches a doctrine that is dependent upon letters and words is a mere prattler, because Truth is beyond letters and words and books.[6]

The central core of Buddhist religiosity does not lie in any objective knowledge or teaching but in the existential realization of truth itself. This is more than intellectual apprehension of a systematic teaching. The *Diamond Sutra* em-

---

[1]*Lankavatara Sutra,* as quoted in Huxley, *op. cit.,* p. 8.

[2]*Sutralamkara,* as quoted in Huxley, *op. cit.,* p. 127.

[3]*Diamond Sutra,* as quoted in Huxley, *op. cit.,* p. 127.

[4]Shih-t'ou, as quoted *ibid.,* p. 127.

[5]*Lankavatara Sutra,* as quoted *ibid.,* p. 133.

[6]*Lankavatara Sutra,* as translated by Dwight Goddard, *A Buddhist Bible* (Thetford, Vermont, 1938), p. 310-311.

phatically cautions against such a misinterpretation of the Buddha's intent:

> The Lord Buddha then warned Subhuti, saying: "Subhuti, do not think that the Tathagata ever considers within his own mind: I ought to ennunciate a system of teaching for the elucidation of the Dharma. You should never cherish such an unworthy thought. And why? Because if any disciple should harbour such a thought, he would not only be misunderstanding the teaching of the Tathagata but he would be slandering him as well. Moreover, what has just been referred to as 'a system of teaching' has no meaning, as Truth cannot be cut up into pieces and arranged into a system. The words can only be used as a figure of speech."[1]

The spiritual life in Buddhism does not lie in any form of information but in enlightenment. Again Buddhism is not a teaching to be adhered to. It cannot be externally conveyed from one person to another as can all the words of the intellect:

> When mind and each believing mind are not divided, and undivided are each believing mind and Mind, This is where words fail,
> For it is not of the past, present or future.[2]

> Buddha asked, "Subodai, What do you think about this: has the Buddha attained to Perfect Enlightenment? Is there any Truth for him to teach?" Subodai answered, "According to the teaching of the Buddha, the World-Honoured One, there is nothing we can call Perfect Enlightenment, neither is there any Truth for the Buddha to teach. Why not? Because we are not to adhere to the teaching of the Buddha, nor is it to be taught."[3]

Enlightenment is not something to have or to give. It is not the result of adding or subtracting.

---

[1] *Diamond Sutra,* as translated *ibid.,* p. 104.
[2] The Third Patriarch of Zen, as quoted in Huxley, *op. cit.,* p. 75.
[3] Diamond Sutra, as quoted in R. H. Blyth, *Zen in English Literature and Oriental Classics* (New York: E. P. Dutton & Co., Inc., 1960), p. 282.

> The human mind possesses the Buddha-nature unobtainable from others. It can be compared to a man who has a jewel in his clothes he knows not of, or to a man who seeks after food when he has a treasure in his own storehouse.[1]

> A special transmission outside of the Scriptures;
> No dependence upon words and letters;
> Direct pointing to the soul of man;
> Seeing into one's nature and the attainment of
> Buddhahood.[2]

The search after God, Reality, Truth or *nirvana* is inseparable from the search after man's own self. In other words, the absolute must never be sought objectively and externally. *Nirvana* is not a place where man's posthumous existence takes place but the human mind in which duality has vanished. *Nirvana* cannot be found apart from the human being's own consciousness, and the quest for reality is a quest of the self for itself.

The quest for true manhood is also most explicitly the sum and substance of the way of Confucius. Avoiding mythology, theology, or metaphysics, the Chinese sage has seemed to many to be only the expounder of a humanistic ethics. But to regard him as only an ethical teacher is to miss his depth. For Confucius, reality is encountered when human relationships are real, and human relationships are only as real as the men who are involved in them. The search for reality is thus a search for true manhood, and this is not the quest of an abstract philosophical ideal but the quest of each for his own true self.

> What Heaven (*T'ien*, Nature) imparts to man is called human nature. To follow our nature is called the Way (Tao). Cultivating the Way is called education. The Way

---

[1] *Surangama Sutra,* as quoted in B. L. Suzuki, *Mahayana Buddhism* (New York: Collier Books, 1963), p. 124.

[2] Quoted from D. T. Suzuki, *Zen Buddhism* (New York: Doubleday & Company, Inc., 1956), p. 9.

cannot be separated from us for a moment. What can be separated from us is not the Way.[1]

To find the Way is to find the core of Confucian religiosity. If one finds the Way, he will have missed nothing. Thus Confucius said:

The Master said, In the morning hear the Way; in the evening, die content![2]

Finding the *tao* or the way necessitates constant effort on man's part. Confucius himself said:

The Master said, A man can enlarge his Way; but there is no Way that can enlarge a man.[3]

In short, as "there are no Buddhas apart from being" so there is no Way apart from man.

Man's relation with other men is for Confucius the vehicle of his relation to the divine. Man's humanity is the window through which he apprehends ultimate reality. Confucius terms the essential core of human relatedness *jen*. Without *jen*, man is unable to be related to other men in terms of mutuality and freedom.

Confucius said, "If a man is not humane (*jen*), what has he to do with ceremonies (*li*)? If he is not humane, what has he to do with music?"[4]

Confucius said, "Only the man of humanity [jen] knows how to love people and hate people."[5]

The master said, Ssu, I believe you look upon me as one whose aim is simply to learn and retain in mind as many things as possible. He replied, That is what I thought. Is it not so? The Master said, No; I have one (thread) upon which I string them all.[6]

[1] *The Doctrine of the Mean*, Ch. 1, as compiled by Wing-tsit Chan, *The Great Asian Religions*, p. 116.

[2] *Analects*, 4:8, as translated in Arthur Waley, *The Analects of Confucius* (New York: A Division of Random House, 1938), p. 103.

[3] *Analects*, 15:28, as translated *ibid.*, p. 199.

[4] *Analects*, 3:3, as compiled by Wing-tsit Chan, *op. cit.*, p. 107.

[5] *Analects*, 4:3, as compiled *ibid.*, p. 107. (Bracketed word is mine.)

[6] *Analects*, 15:2, as translated in Waley, *op. cit.*, p. 193.

Yen Hui said with a deep sigh, the more I strain my
gaze up towards it, the higher it soars. The deeper I bore
down into it, the harder it becomes. I see it in front; but
suddenly it is behind. Step by step the Master skilfully
lures one on. He has broadened me with culture, re-
strained me with ritual. Even if I wanted to stop, I could
not. Just when I feel that I have exhausted every resource,
something seems to rise up, standing out sharp and clear.
Yet though I long to pursue it, I can find no way of getting
to it at all.[1]

These citations show that the true human relatedness is
not merely ethical but also religious. In other words, true
human relatedness is not merely a relation between man
and man, but also a relation between man, Heaven and
earth. "The true man can find himself in no situation in
which he is not at ease with himself." [2] There is no need to
find a specific place and time in order to find the divine or
the ultimate. There is no place where the ultimate can be
hidden. Confucius himself said:

Confucius said, "How abundant is the display of power
of spiritual beings! We look for them but do not see them.
We listen to them but do not hear them. They form the substance of all things and nothing can be without them. . . .
Such is the manifestation of the subtle. Such is the impossibility of hiding the real (ch'eng)."[3]

The way to find the ultimate is not to seek it without but to
enquire within. Pedagogically, one may begin by enquiring
of objective doctrines or teachings, but he cannot end with
objective knowledge. Objective knowledge has its own
validity, only when it leads man to enquire within. Man's
whole life must be devoted to such a searching for true
self.

[1] *Analects*, 9:10, as translated *ibid.*, p. 140.
[2] *The Doctrine of the Mean*, Ch. 14, as compiled in Wing-tsit Chan, *op. cit.*, p. 116.
[3] *Ibid.*, p. 116.

> The Master said, At fifteen I set my heart upon learn-
> ing. At thirty, I had planted my feet firm upon the ground.
> At forty, I no longer suffered from perplexities. At fifty, I
> knew what were the biddings of Heaven. At sixty, I heard
> them with docile ear. At seventy, I could follow the dic-
> tates of my own heart; for what I desired no longer over-
> stepped the boundaries of right.[1]

Confucianism is religion and not ethics alone, since it seeks
for an ultimate grounding of human life. It is a response to
finitude which approaches the infinitude through the realization of human-heartedness or *jen*. The deepest meaning
of *jen* is the non-duality of self and other, and the cultivation of *jen* is the development of a non-dualistic relationship to the whole of life. Man without *jen* is alienated from
life. Man with *jen* is one with life. It is thus religious oneness with life that is the goal of Confucianism and the exploration of its full meaning is the content of Confucian
theory and practice. Purification of one's own heart is
opening to reality. Sincerity in Confucius is not merely a
human virtue; it is the existential condition of any ontology
which is more than the playing with abstractions:

> Only those who are absolutely sincere can fully develop
> their nature. If they can fully develop their nature, they can
> then fully develop the nature of others. If they can fully de-
> velop the nature of others, they can then fully develop the
> nature of things. If they can then fully develop the nature
> of things, they can then assist in the transforming and nour-
> ishing process of Heaven and Earth. If they can assist in
> the transforming and nourishing process of Heaven and
> Earth, they can thus form a trinity with Heaven and
> Earth.[2]

> Sincerity means the completion of the self, and the Way
> is self-directing. Sincerity is the beginning and end of
> things. Without sincerity there would be nothing. There-
> fore the superior man values sincerity. Sincerity is not only
> the completion of one's own self; it is that by which all

[1]*Analects*, 2:4, as translated in Waley, *op. cit.,* p. 88.
[2]*The Doctrine of the Mean*, Ch. 22, as compiled in Wing-tsit Chan *et al.,*
The Great Asian Religions, p. 117.

things are completed. The completion of all things means wisdom. These are the character of the nature, and they are the Way in which the internal and the external are united. Therefore whenever it is employed, everything done is right.

Therefore absolute sincerity is ceaseless. Being ceaseless, it is lasting. Being lasting, it is evident. Being evident, it is infinite, it is extensive and deep. Being extensive and deep, it is high and brilliant. It is because it is extensive and deep that it contains all things. It is because it is high and brilliant that it overshadows all things. It is because it is infinite and lasting that it can complete all things. In being extensive and deep, it is a counterpart of Earth. In being high and brilliant, it is counterpart of Heaven. In being infinite and lasting, it is unlimited. Such being its nature, it becomes prominent without any display, produces changes without motion, and accomplishes its ends without action. . . [1]

Taoism is no more objectifiable than is Confucianism. It is utterly alien to its central spirituality to view it as a conformity to propositions which may be analyzed by a scientific researcher. And while many have viewed it only as a quietistic religion, to regard it as such is to miss its depth, even as it would be to interpret it as a kind of antinomianism. For Taoism, the deed is real when the doer is real. The search for truth in action is thus the search for truth in being. Thus Taoism is neither on the side of sheer objectivity nor on that of sheer subjectivity. By the same token it is neither oriented toward ethical activity nor is it quietistic. In short, it is beyond dualism.

There is no technique or formula for opening oneself to ultimate reality. Formula yields forms, not realities. Lao-Tzu terms the ultimate reality of man's life *tao*.

The Tâo that can be trodden is not the enduring and unchanging Tâo. The name that can be named is not the enduring and unchanging name.[2]

[1] *The Doctrine of the Mean,* Ch. 25 and Ch. 26, as compiled *ibid.,* p. 117.
[2] *The Texts of Taoism* (Translated by James Legge and introduced by D. T. Suzuki) (New York: The Julian Press, 1959), Ch. 1.1., p. 95.

(Conceived of as) having no name, it is the Originator of heaven and earth; (conceived of as) having a name, it is the Mother of all things.[1]

We look at it, and we do not see it, and we name it 'the Equable.' We listen to it, and we do not hear it, and we name it 'the inaudible.' We try to grasp it, and do not get hold of it, and we name it 'the Subtle.' With these three qualities, it cannot be made the subject of description; and hence we blend them together and obtain The One.[2]

Its upper part is not bright, and its lower part is not obscure. Ceaseless in its action, it yet cannot be named, and then it again returns and becomes nothing. This is called the Form of the Formless, and the Semblance of the Invisible; this is called the Fleeting and Indeterminable.[3]

We meet it and do not see its Front; we follow it, and do not see its Back. When we can lay hold of the Tâo of old and direct the things of the present day, and are able to know it as it was of old in the beginning, this is called (unwinding) the clue of Tâo.[4]

The way or *tao* is thus formless and nameless in the sense that its infinite living being is not captured or exhausted by any form or any description. In other words, it is formless or nameless, simply because it cannot be objectified. This does not mean that *tao* transcends true manhood. On the contrary, it is so closely related to man's true self as to be hardly distinguishable from it:

To him who holds in his hands the Great Image (of the invisible Tâo), the whole world repairs. Men resort to him, and receive no hurt, but (find) rest, peace, and the feeling of ease.[5]

Music and dainties will make the passing guest stop (for a time). But though the Tâo as it comes from the mouth, seems insipid and has no flavour, though it seems

[1]*Ibid.*, Ch. 1.2., p. 95.
[2]*Ibid.*, Ch. 14.1., p. 105.
[3]*Ibid.*, Ch. 14.2., p. 105.
[4]*Ibid.*, Ch. 14.3., p. 105.
[5]*Ibid.*, Ch. 35.1, p. 125.

not worth being looked at or listened to, the use of it is in-exhaustible.[1]

Thus, the formlessness or namelessness of *tao* is its non-objectivity. It follows that *tao* is not to be sought externally, but existentially:

He who knows other men is discerning; he who knows himself is intelligent.[2]

When reality or truth is taken to be external to the self, that truth can never become wholly natural to the self; it will always be felt as a superimposition upon the self and will thereby always engender resistance. Taoism seeks a truth that is perfectly natural, that is not imposed from without on one's own nature. "Be natural" in Taoism means "Be your true self or be truly yourself." The Taoist sage is the perfectly natural man who has found the true self in which he can be wholly at ease. In short, he is one with Confucius who can do whatever his heart desires without doing wrong:

The Tâo in its regular course does nothing (for the sake of doing it), and so there is nothing which it does not do.[3]

If princes and kings were able to maintain it, all things would of themselves by transformed by them.[4]

If this transformation became to me an object of desire, I would express the desire by the nameless simplicity.

Simplicity without a name
Is free from all external aim.
With no desire, at rest and still,
All things go right as of their will.[5]

Without going outside his door, one understands (all that takes place) under the sky; without looking out from his window, one sees the Tâo of Heaven. The farther that one goes out (from himself), the less he knows.[6]

[1]*Ibid.*, Ch. 35.2., p. 125.
[2]*Ibid.*, Ch. 33.1., p. 123.
[3]*Ibid.*, Ch. 37.1., p. 127.
[4]*Ibid.*, Ch. 37.2., p. 127.
[5]*Ibid.*, Ch. 37. 3., p. 127.
[6]*Ibid.*, Ch. 47. 1., p. 137.

Therefore the sages got their knowledge without travel-
ling; gave their (right) names to things without seeing
them; and accomplished their ends without any purpose of
doing so.[1]

The truly natural self is not to be sought as an external
goal. It is not to be gained, but it is to be found within:

He who devotes himself to learning (seeks) from day to
day to increase (his knowledge); he who devotes himself to
the Tâo (seeks) from day to day to diminish (his doing).[2]

The real meaning of these words is that loss is not opposed
to gain. By the same token, rest in this context cannot be
opposed to activity. Rather it goes beyond both passivity
and activity.

Taoism terms the essential core of rest *wu-wei*. *Wu-wei*
cannot merely be translated into non-action which seems to
be opposed to action. It really means non-duality of doer
and deed, where the doer does not impose himself on the
deed, where the form does no violence to the material.
Where the doer and the deed are inwardly related, there
one has *wu-wei*. Otherwise the doer is either too big for the
deed and appears like an intruder, or the deed is too big
for the doer and he is dragged along by it. Thus *wu-wei* is
neither a kind of doing nor a kind of non-doing. It is a way
of being at one with the action.

That which is at rest is easily kept hold of; before a
thing has given indications of its presence, it is easy to take
measures against it; that which is brittle is easily broken;
that which is very small is easily dispersed. Action should
be taken before a thing has made its appearance; order
should be secured before disorder has begun.[3]

The tree which fills the arms grew from the tiniest
sprout; the tower of nine storeys rose from a (small) heap
of earth; the journey of a thousand li commenced with a
single step.[4]

[1] *Ibid.*, Ch. 47. 2., p. 137.
[2] *Ibid.*, Ch. 48. 1., p. 138.
[3] *Ibid.*, Ch. 64. 1., pp. 155-156.
[4] *Ibid.*, Ch. 64. 2., pp. 155-156.

He who acts (with an ulterior purpose) does harm; he who takes hold of a thing (in the same way) loses his hold. The sage does not act (so), and therefore does no harm; he does not lay hold (so), and therefore does not lose his hold. (But) people in their conduct of affairs are constantly ruining them when they are on the eve of success. If they were careful at the end, as (they should be) at the beginning, they would not so ruin them.[1]

Therefore the sage desires what (other men) do not desire, and does not prize things difficult to get; he learns what (other men) do not learn, and turns back to what the multitude of men have passed by. Thus he helps the natural development of all things, and does not dare to act (with an ulterior purpose of his own).[2]

In similar vein, we find Chuang Tzu saying:

The stillness of the sages does not belong to them as a consequence of their skilful ability; all things are not able to disturb their minds;—it is on this account that they are still.[3]

Therefore while the actions of the Great Man are not directed to injure men, he does not plume himself on his benevolence and kindness; while his movements are not made with a view to gain, he does not consider the menials of a family as mean; while he does not strive after property and wealth, he does not plume himself on declining them; while he does not borrow the help of others to accomplish his affairs, he does not plume himself on supporting himself by his own strength, nor does he despise those who in their greed do what is mean; while he differs in his conduct from the vulgar, he does not plume himself on being so different from them; while it is his desire to follow the multitude, he does not despise the glib-tongued flatterers. The rank and emoluments of the world furnish no stiumulus to him, nor does he reckon its punishments and shame to be disgrace. He knows that the right and the wrong can (often) not be distinguished, and that what is small and what is great can (often) not be defined. I have heard it said, "The man of Tâo does not become distinguished; the

[1] *Ibid.,* Ch. 64. 3., pp. 155-156.
[2] *Ibid.,* Ch. 64. 4., pp. 155-156.
[3] Chuang-tzu, Bk. xiii. 1., p. 378.

greatest virtue is unsuccessful; the Great Man has no thought of self";—to so great a degree may the lot be restricted.'[1]

Whatever has form, semblance, sound, and colour is a thing; how can one thing come to be different from another? But it is not competent for any of these things to reach to what preceded them all;—they are but (form and) visibility. But (the perfect man) attains to be (as it were) without form, and beyond the capability of being transformed. Now when one attains to this and carries it out to the highest degree, how can other things come into his way to stop him? He will occupy the place assigned to him without going beyond it, and lie concealed in the clue which has no end. He will study with delight the process which gives their beginning and ending to all things. By gathering his nature into a unity, by nourishing his vital power, by concentrating his virtue, he will penetrate to the making of things. In this condition, with his heavenly constitution kept entire, and with no crevice in his Spirit, how can things enter (and disturb his serenity)?[2]

The child will cry all the day, without its throat becoming hoarse;—so perfect is the harmony (of its physical constitution). It will keep its fingers closed all the day without relaxing their grasp;—such is the concentration of its powers. It will keep its eyes fixed all day, without their moving;—so is it unaffected by what is external to it. It walks it knows not whither; it rests where it is placed, it knows not why; it is calmly indifferent to things, and follows their current. This is the regular method of guarding the life.'[3]

If one who has not this entire sincerity in himself makes any outward demonstration, every such demonstration will be incorrect. The thing will enter into him, and not let go its hold. Then with every fresh demonstration there will be still greater failure. If he does what is not good in the light of open day, men will have the opportunity of punishing him; if he does it in darkness and secrecy, spirits will inflict the punishment. Let a man understand this—his relation both

---

[1]*Ibid.*, Bk. xvii. 3., pp. 426-427.
[2]*Ibid.*, Bk. xix. 2., p. 453.
[3]*Ibid.*, Bk. xxiii. 5., pp. 520-521.

to men and spirits, and then he will do what is good in the solitude of himself.[1]

To return to non-action or *wu-wei*, therefore, is not to return to quietism, but to return to the ultimate ground of life which is the root of both activity and passivity. For Taoism the root of both activity and passivity is no other than man, who is the doer. He is called a sage whose life is not divorced from his actions and in whom the inner and the outer are a unity. The sage's life is the undivided life or the integral life, and his naturalness means that he is living from his whole nature, which is itself not divorced from the nature of things. Thus, his life is not merely quietistic but fundamentally ontological.

In summary, then, oriental spirituality whether in its Hindu, Buddhist, Confucianist or Taoist forms would seem to encompass a quest after something which cannot be communicated by words. What is communicated by words is what is definable in languages, and that which is defined is fixed in a specific place and time. Thus, it can be said that what is communicated is what can be limited to a specific place and time. Accordingly one can achieve that which can be communicated, and he can possess its truth. But only dead things can be possessed; life is not to be possessed. It can be lived but not owned. It must be allowed to move; it cannot be held, simply because finite knowledge finishes life, and such knowledge pertains to abstractions or limited portions of objectified life. Living truth has got to be unfinished, undefined, i.e., infinite truth.

Thus many of the teachings of oriental sages are not teachings in the ordinary sense, that is, collections of ideas which purport to convey truth. They are provisional and pedagogical and meant to function as fingers pointing to the moon. To take what has been written down as truth is like taking a finger as the moon. What is set down is only a single crystal drawn from an infinite matrix which is eternally fluid. It is our contention that the highest wisdom of

---

[1]*Ibid.*, Bk. xxiii. 8., p. 523.

the orient seeks to tap the matrix and not simply to collect crystals.

If one takes doctrines or teachings as truth, then one is divorced from infinite truth. To be separated from Truth means to adhere to truths. To limit oneself to objective knowledge is to be rational, intellectual, or abstract. And this is to be abstracted from one's whole being. Then, life is lived abstractly. As a result of living abstractly, truths—which are gained by human intellect—take precedence over human existence as a whole. In other words, a portion of man's existence takes hegemony over the whole.

The spiritual quest as suggested by the passages cited is a search for wholeness or integrity of being and this can never be mediated through any portion of man—either by reason or feeling or faith or knowledge, nor is it given through obedience (e.g., to the will of God), nor through any conformity with the law or will of another, nor by imitating the life of another. Conformity yields only formality, not reality. No man can enter into the Truth, unless he himself realizes the Truth. Apart from his own realization of the ultimate Truth, no amount of belief or conformity can be religious in the ultimate sense of the word.

In the last analysis, we would claim oriental religiosity does not subject the human to the divine, nor does it see the divine as simply derivative from the human; they seek to heal the dichotomy between the divine and the human and this is not achieved when either is subordinated to the other.

Realization of Truth is actualized to the extent that man experiences his life as not different from Truth itself. Truth cannot be sought apart from life itself, which means finally my own life. A truth which gives the alternatives of acceptance or rejection cannot be the truth of one's own being where submission or rebellion are possible. It is the thesis of this essay that the spiritual goal of oriental religiosity lies not in yielding life to Truth but in experiencing the infinite Truth of life itself.

Since Truth is not separated from life itself, it is not

amenable to an objective transmission. It is not a commodity of any kind. Man is made to be human in the truest sense of the word. Apart from being truly human, all man's activity is in the wrong track, if his seeking is separated from his own life. A truly religious man as depicted in the sacred literature of the orient lives the Truth in his own life. His self-identity is Truth, and Truth is his identity. Thus his task is no other than his life. In this respect, no man can be religious, unless he enters into his own life. Religion, therefore, is a fundamental quest or search for one's true life, and this quest for true self is no other than the search for Truth itself.

This Truth has not in the orient been conceived of simply as a posthumous state of being. Nor is it simply equated with the fulfillment of the finite potentialities of human life. Neither a supernaturalistic nor a naturalistic nor a humanistic rendering does justice to it. It is most nearly described as a realization of infinity in finitude, as an absolute fulfillment of life here-now. This is variously designated as realization, liberation or enlightenment, and he who achieves it is called a *sage,* a *buddha,* a *chun-tzu,* a *man of tao* or *jivanmukta.*

Enlightenment has to do with man's wholeness in the midst of his finite life. For oriental spirituality the problem is how man becomes one with his own life or how he moves from endeavoring to cope with it from an external position to being inside of it. Becoming one with his own life is entirely different from abstractly knowing his finitude, and subordinating himself to an infinite deemed to be outside himself. The difference is not in degree but in kind. The religious goal of the orient lies not in choosing any portion of life, but in being one with life itself. Enlightenment lies not in any form of life but in life itself.

Life itself, unlike a portion of life, is not possessed-life but lived-life. To express it differently: it is enlightenment that life itself is not of man but in man and he is in it. Man's true life is not merely the limited thing he calls his own but fundamentally infinite life.

It becomes clear that the expression "my life," "your life," "its life" or "his life" from the ultimate standpoint is a kind of obscenity. To reduce life to one's own possession is a violation of the living mystery. To live in this living mystery is to realize the living paradox which is the core of oriental religiosity, the non-duality of finite and infinite, of the individual and *brahman* or *tao* or the *buddha*. These are but different names for the one living mystery. As the *Vedas* puts it, "Truth is one; sages call it by different names." It cannot be possessed, and thus it cannot be experienced as an object. Rather it lives in all beings and they in it. That which is experienced as an object is that which is abstracted from Life itself. Seen from this point of view, possessed-life is abstract life. What is lost in the abstract life is Life itself, and thus abstract life becomes meaningless, alienated or dead.

Thus, to search for true life or true manhood is not merely a humanistic but ultimately a cosmic search. Since the goal of religion, in the oriental sense of the word, is not separated from man's life, the quest for Truth or Being or Ultimacy is no other than the search for Life itself. Life itself is not separated from both man's own life and Truth itself. In Life itself, the ultimate is not divorced from the immediate, and the human is not separated from the natural. In other words, all opposites are combined in Life itself, and he who finds life becomes a "cosmic man."

Life itself can neither be understood nor achieved by any analysis of the human being. What is yielded by analytic methods are abstracted portions of man's life. Man's life is not merely emotional, nor merely intellectual, nor merely volitional. It is true manhood that man both encompasses and transcends his biological, psychological, philosophical, or sociological dimensions. The cosmic or religious quest for true manhood seeks to relate one's self with one's alienated-self, and the latter comprises other selves, nature and the divine as well. In other words, the cosmic quest for true manhood lies in seeing the relatedness of man's life and infinite life itself or in perceiving the unity of the seeker and the sought.

The contention of this dissertation, then, is that the relatedness of seeker and sought is the key without which one cannot open the door to the *sanctum sanctorum* of oriental spirituality, which contains a living and saving Truth neither rational nor irrational, neither theoretical nor passionate, neither abstract nor concrete, neither personal nor impersonal, and not to be apprehended either by logic or by faith. It transcends all these dichotomies, and is the source of true life. To actualize it in the seeker is the ultimate aim of oriental religiosity.

The attempt to characterize the religious thought of the orient by limiting oneself to objective analysis is tantamount to dissecting a corpse in order to apprehend its life. What this yields is anatomical structure and not functioning life.

The following four chapters attempt to review some recent interpretations of oriental religiosity. The first chapter is an evaluation of some recent attempts to deal with oriental religious culture as a whole and to distill its essence. The following three chapters focus on the three major traditions of Hinduism, Buddhism, Confucianism and Taoism as dealt with respectively.

CHAPTER II

THE MEETING OF THE TWAIN

It will deepen our understanding of the essential spirit of oriental religiosity if we set our preliminary characterization of it alongside a number of others recently attempted by both occidental and oriental scholars. Indeed, there are many eminent scholars—William Ernest Hocking, F. S. C. Northrop, Hajime Nakamura, Fung Yu-lan, Bhagavan Das, and Allan Watts among others,—who have sought to grasp the basic thrust of the religious consciousness of the orient. In appearance at least, our characterization of it may seem to be fundamentally similar to some of theirs. I hope to make plain, however, the fundamental oversight which is present to a greater or lesser degree in virtually all such attempts.

For most occidentals, one of the major obstacles to grasping the focal intent of oriental spirituality is the lack of anything to grasp. Amorphousness and illogicality have seemed to many to be its most apparent traits. To the mind nurtured in clarity of concept, and loyalty to a clearly defined tradition, it is incomprehensible how a Chinese, for example, can be both a Confucianist and a Taoist, even as he also uses the services of a Buddhist priest on some occasions, and on still others, participates in purely primitive rituals.

Some scholars have accepted this kind of indifference to logical consistency as a psychological or cultural difference between the orient and the occident and have abstained from applying occidental canons to oriental religion without, however, perceiving its deeper inwardness. One of them is William Ernest Hocking who wrote *Living Religions and a World Faith*. In this book, Hocking has interpreted many of the world religions, both living and bygone, and discussed both present and future attitudes towards them. And finally he has formulated his own estimate of the prospects of Christianity as a world faith.

The philosophy behind the book is neither dogmatic particularism on the one hand, nor, on the other, a universalism which surmounts all particularity of faith. His aim is to accept all religions, to preserve his own Christian commitment, and to be sensitive to the spirit of religion which pervades all particular forms. He has to confront the ancient problem of the universal and the particular as it affects religions:

> This is a wholly new question. It is radically different in its motive and urgency from that of the religious mission. The mission tries to make a particular religion universal. The new interest is to escape particularity and localism, finding in religions what is already universal. The urgency behind it is not that of the propagandist, but that of world citizenship. There is a universal science; there should be universal law; why may we not also expect a world faith?[1]

In this spirit of world citizenship, Hocking has tried to understand other religious ideas. The spirit is well expressed in the following statement:

> And it is a question which carries its own answer, an affirmative; if there is to be a world culture, and if there is to be any such thing as religion in the new order, there must be a world faith. In that sharp light, all one's localisms are seen to be local, and therefore unessential, relative, queer, afflicted with the staleness of ancient subjectivities, like a stuffy air which one can no longer endure to breathe once one has been outside in the freshness of a great morning. God is in his world, but Buddha, Jesus, Mohammed are in their little private closets, and we shall thank them, but

[1]William Ernest Hocking, *Living Religions and a World Faith* (New York: Macmillan Co., 1940), p. 21.

never return to them. Such is the spirit of world citizenship at this moment.[1]

In the same vein, Hocking has emphasized that oriental religions are not to be approached as packages of local news, and furthermore not as packages of facts or teachings:

> . . . we are not likely to dispose of any of these religions by showing it to be in error: An oriental religion is extraordinarily hard to refute! It is not that the standard of truth and falsity fails to apply to the dogmas of religion. It is that a religion cannot in general be identified with a doctrinal position.[2]

In other words, Hocking sees clearly that oriental religions do not have the definiteness of creedal positions. They are directed toward man's total liberation and are not aimed at pleasing his intellect alone. Doctrines, whether theological or metaphysical, are important only as preliminaries to liberation and realization, and apart from inner realization, all doctrinal formulations are considered as secondary and external to the truth. Accordingly, the goal is to enact the ultimate truth in one's own immediate being and not to find an external truth to adhere to.

Hocking has also perceived that in consequence, oriental religions are extraordinarily pliant:

> These religions can bend and alter without breaking. Their relative formlessness and deficiency in organization, together with their capacity just now dwelt on for absorbing new ideas into their structure, tends to enable them to survive when by most signs they should be ready to perish.[3]

Hocking has understood this plasticity of the oriental religious spirit to a degree:

> Yet it lies in the nature of the case that the more successful, masterly and profound the expositions, the less do they prepare the mind for the actual Oriental scene.[4]

[1] *Ibid.*, pp. 22-23.
[3] *Ibid.*, p. 118.
[3] *Ibid.*, p. 67.
[4] *Ibid.*, p. 67.

For no religion, Oriental or other, can be identified with a
metaphysical position; nor can the issues between them be
stated in such terms.[1]

We see, then why it is not alone natural but sound that a
Chinese should be a Confucianist and also a Buddhist; the
one performs the particular and local functions of religions, the other the universal and transcendent functions.
So long as no one religion does both, two religions are likely to be better than one.[2]

But while sociological, philosophical, psychological
and other explanations have some validity, they do not go
deep enough. May it not be that the flexibility of the oriental mind is ontologically grounded, that is, is the result
of the nature of that reality which is the goal of the religious quest as the orient conceives of it? May it not be
that the psychological and cultural traits derive from a
sense for reality which is not imprisoned by self-imposed
canons of logical clarity? Why should one deprive oneself
of the nourishment available in other traditions simply
out of a sense of exclusive loyalty to one attempt to pin the
absolute down in words? Hocking concedes that what is
an outstanding puzzle to occidentals may be the expression
of sound instinct in the oriental:

There is the maximum difference in ritual and folklore, but
the maximum likeness in ideas, the underlying conceptions
and the attitudes are everywhere the same.[3]

That all religious formulations without exception are
merely provisonal and pedagogical in character, that they
lack intrinsic or ultimate significance, that they do not con-
tain the absolute, that it is folly to cling to them and to war
over them, that liberation comes only from reality and not
from words which inadequately seek to convey it—this is
the ontological import of that quality of plasticity which
Hocking has pointed to without fully understanding its

[1]*Ibid.,* p. 100.
[2]*Ibid.,* p. 77.
[3]*Ibid.,* p. 89.

meaning. In other words, the orient evinces a truly spiritual grasp of spiritual realities; it does not confuse the bottle and the wine and it has always understood that "the letter killeth and the spirit giveth life" and that because "God is spirit; He must be worshipped in spirit and in truth."

Thus, it is not proper to ask of an oriental religion "What does it teach concerning . . . ?" Its aim is not to present a replica of reality in the form of a teaching. It teaches what it has to teach to enable the seeker to find himself on a deeper level. It will use any replica and eventually discard every replica. Its teaching at any level is a provisional adaptation to the level of the seeker at that moment. It is not an ultimate rendering of truth.

Herein is to be found a much deeper basis for religious pluralism and tolerance. For the orient these are ontological necessities: "Truth is one, but the sages call it by many names." A pluralism of pedagogies is inevitable. As any object may be viewed from multiple perspectives and as a mountain may be scaled from different sides, so the approaches to the absolute are not limited in number. To the oriental mind, the ideal of one shepherd and one flock is incomprehensible. It reduces living truth to an abstraction, religion to a quasi-mathematical system, and reality to a verbal formulation. Tolerance towards other formulations and participation in a plurality of traditions is, to the orient, not merely social courtesy or a moral value, but an ontological necessity.

Consequently, what is nowadays called *ecumenism,* has also a much deeper meaning in the religious awareness of the orient. There it is not seen as an ecclesiological desideratum, but as an existential condition of authentic spirituality. The universal truth has to be realized in man's own existence, and the existential approach to this truth requires an ecumenism which involves all that one is and not simply one's identity as a member of a particular religion (which can never be one's ultimate identity). The external, purely organizational and non-existential approach to ecumenism has not revealed its true spirit. To the oriental mind, the existential realization of the absolute is the ultimate truth of the religious life. Therefore, true ecumenism to the oriental mind is neither objectivism nor subjectivism, but a movement towards the absolute. In this respect, Hocking's ecumenism is perhaps qualified by an untranscended particularism:

> Everyone must be honest with himself, not surrendering his faith or softening down his convictions, but outspoken and sincere, holding to what he believed to be the truth and ready to declare it, and yet maintaining a tolerant and open mind.[1]

For the orient, this is good but not good enough.

F. S. C. Northrop is no less sympathetic towards oriental religions than is Hocking, but his universalism is of a more abstract sort. In his *The Meeting of East and West,* Northrop has tried to resolve theoretically the sources of conflict between East and West:

> It is hardly likely that these sources of conflict can be faced and removed *in practice* within the halls of parliaments and the heated actions of the market place, where slogans are carelessly bandied about, speical interests are at work, and passions are easily aroused, unless the problems raised are first traced to their roots and then resolved *in theory* within the calmness of the study where the meaning of words like "democracy" and "communism" can be carefully determined and the issues which they define can be looked at more objectively. It is with this timely, important and difficult understanding that this book is concerned, as its sub-title indicates.[2]

He attempts to enumerate the difference between the orient and the occident in terms of their differing ideological assumptions. Although he recognizes a plurality of oriental cultures, Northrop is primarily concerned with ascertaining the essential resemblances between them:

---

[1]*Ibid.,* p. 272.

[2]F. S. C. Northrop, *The Meeting of East and West* (New York: The Macmillan Company, 1947), pp. ix-x.

> Nevertheless, to specify these facts which distinguish one country or culture from the others is at the same time to indicate the equally evident interconnections and identities which tie them all together to constitute a single civilization of the East. . . . Confucius, for all his originality, continuously insisted that he obtained his wisdom from a laborious study of the ancient classics. Lao-Tzu, the founder of Taoism, went back to the ancient classics also. Moreover, as will be shown, what he found there is precisely what the Buddha found in the ancient classics of the civilizations of India. Similarly, the founder of Buddhism claimed no originality, but insisted instead that he was returning a corrupted or overlaid Hinduism to its original source in the poetry to the early Upanishads and the even earlier Vedic hymns. . . . Thus, to specify the philosophical and religious differences entering into the constitution of the cultures of the East is at the same time to possess inescapable interconnections and identities. It is the unity provided by these essential relations and identities which merges the cultures of the Oriental countries into one traditional culture of the Far East.[1]

Thus for Northrop, the *East* signifies a cultural unity, and the ancient insights of its peoples are variations on a theme. This he interprets as follows:

> The oriental asserts the primary factor in human nature and the nature of all things to be something which neither the formal methods of science and philosophy nor determinate qualities can convey; and uses logically formulated doctrines, without contradiction, either positively to lead one toward the primary indescribable factor or else negatively to designate what the primary factor in the nature of things is not.[2]

In his own way, Northrop perceives oriental spirituality as something which cannot be communicated by words, reason, or doctrines:

> It is to be emphasized that in the entire process no knowl-

[1]*Ibid.*, pp. 312-313.
[2]*Ibid.*, p. 365.

edge or application of theoretically formulated, scientif-
ically verified, postulationally prescribed theory, either in itself or in its applications, is required.[1]

But this perception is still within the context of duality and
he sees oriental spirituality as centered around that which
is opposed to reason:

> For the Indian, and for the Oriental generally, as for the
> Western Spaniard, emotion or passion is of the essence of
> human nature and of the divine nature.[2]

> The Oriental portion of the world has concentrated its at-
> tention upon the nature of all things in their emotional and
> aesthetic, purely empirical and positivistic immediacy.[3]

Again, from the oriental point of view, he goes astray in
conceiving of the ultimate as standing in opposition to
something other, in short, as one of two.

> . . . That the undifferentiated, emotionally or passionately
> moving, ineffable aesthetic continuum which we have
> shown also to be what is menat by *tao, jen, Nirvana,* and
> *Brahman,* is often referred to throughout all Oriental reli-
> gions, as the fema . principle.[4]

Since female is only the counterpart to male, how can it
partake of ultimacy to the exclusion of its counterpart?
This is the dualistic error of choosing one pole of an opposition as more real than the other. For the highest oriental
religious consciousness, truth is not defined by opposition.
The truly absolute does not stand over against anything. It
is not female as against male, nor emotional as against rational, nor immediated as against postulated, nor aesthetic
as against theoretical. Northrop correctly proclaims the
underlying unity of oriental religious culture, but fails to
grasp its true nature. Both his perception and his misperception are expressed in the following paragraph:

[1]*Ibid.,* p. 317.
[2]*Ibid.,* p. 371.
[3]*Ibid.,* p. 375.
[4]*Ibid.,* pp. 371-372.

> It appears that jen in Confucianism, Tao in Taoism, Nirvana in Buddhism and Brahman or Atman or Chit in Hinduism and Jainism are all to be identified with the immediately apprehended aesthetic components in the nature of things, and with this in its all-embracing indeterminateness, after all sensed distinctions are abstracted. Evidently Oriental civilization has a single predominant meaning.[1]

According to Northrop, the immediately apprehended aesthetic components are not only the chief characteristic of oriental culture but also the ultimate of oriental religiosity. Northrop says:

> The religious and philosophical ultimate of the East has no determinate attribute whatever.[2]

He sees clearly that oriental religiosity is not directed towards anything objectively describable. He relates it to man's aesthetic experience rather than his theoretic reasoning. It is not by his reason that man contacts the prime essential, but in the immediacy of experience. For Northrop, it is intuition which is at the core of oriental religiosity:

> The ultimate of the East can only be intuited and contemplated.[3]

> Man in the orient cannot be saved by the doctrine or the faith but by intuition and contemplation.[4]

> A concept by intuition is one which denotes, and the complete meaning of which is given by something which is immediately apprehended.[5]

In other words, Northrop sees clearly that the pearl of great price of oriental religions cannot be found externally

---

[1]*Ibid.*, p. 374.

[2]Edited in C. A. Moore, "The Complementary Emphases of Eastern Intuitive and Western Scientific Philosophy," ed. *Philosophy-East and West* (Princeton: Princeton University Press, 1944), p. 219.

[3]Northrop, *The Meeting of East and West*, p. 219.

[4]*Ibid.*, p. 220.

[5]Northrop, "The Complementary Emphases of Eastern Intuitive and Western Scientific Philosophy," *Philosophy—East and West*, ed. by Charles A. Moore, p. 173.

but intuitively. This he takes to signify that these religions are fundamentally aesthetic:

> Forthwith the ineffable, emotional, aesthetic luminosity which is immediately experienced in oneself and nature is restored to the essential nature of all things.[1]

Thus Northrop attempts to set up oriental religions as the counterpart to occidental religions, the one emphasizing the ineffable, aesthetic, emotional dimension and the other the articulatable, theoretic, rational dimension. In this way, he sees each as the complement of the other.

That Northrop seems determined to reconcile East and West as the twin foci of a philosophical system which he had worked out before undertaking the task of reconciliation is not the main objection to be made at this juncture. It is more important to note that Northrop's grasp of the goal and method of the oriental religious consciousness is purely dualistic. Throughout his discussion, the postulated stands in opposition to *immediately given, emotion* is contrasted to *intellect,* and *intuition* with *reason.* He is caught in the play of these and other dichotomies, and he shows no awareness of the elemental urge of the orient to be delivered from such fissuring and to attain to a reality in which life is whole and not divided between opposites.

When oriental religiosity turns away from *A* as a satisfactory *terminus ad quem* of the spiritual quest, that does not mean it is turning towards *Not-A.* For the dualistic consciousness, the negation of A is the affirmation of not-A, and vice versa. So that if reason is not the way, then intuition is the way, etc. One thing is always being set over against the other. But for the orient, it is *neti, neti,* not *this,* not *that*—or in other words "A plague on both your houses." Reality is not one of two and never to be found in the realm of opposition. Going from one pole to its opposite is remaining on the plane of relativity. One reaches

[1]Northrop, *The Meeting of East and West,* p. 450.

absoluteness by transcending the opposition, and this is something Northrop totally fails to grasp.

Northrop's interpretation of oriental religious ideas has some validity, but he does not seem to us to penetrate into their real depth. Intuition in the highest sense is not the experience of reality as "aesthetic luminosity" but the perception of the non-duality of seer and seen. It opens man to a reality which is not confined by an individual experience that is sensory. To the orient, intuition is the union of a whole human being and the intuited. Intuition thus is not opposed to reason, and does not deny it, nor is it on the side of emotion; rather it includes and transcends both. To the oriental mind, intuition is not to be separated from Reality, Truth, Being, or Ultimacy. Thus, it has its cosmic meaning. In other words, intuition is to the orient not merely intuition, but fundamentally Intuition.

Liberation, as the orient conceives of it, as the ultimate goal of human life, comes only from cosmic intuition and not from any sensory insight. The orient does not confuse ordinary empirical intuition and cosmic intuition, and it has always understood that the ultimate cannot be experienced as an indeterminate X but as Being itself.

Being itself cannot be characterized either as *immanent* or transcendent, and it is wrong to identify it as Northrop does with *immediacy*—as it is also wrong of him to identify *transcendent* with *postulated*. Cosmic intuition grasps Being prior to its division into *immanent* and *transcendent*.

To say that the ultimate cannot be found in duality is to reject any characterization of it by either of any pair of polar opposites. The idea of Being as transcendent is as incomprehensible to the highest oriental religious consciousness as the idea of Being as purely immanent. The former overemphasizes the transcendence of the absolute within all beings. The latter overemphasizes the immanence of the ultimate and does not take in its transcendental aspect. The former reduces man's life to a thing of lesser worth, while the latter identifies man's limited self with the ultimate. Cosmic intuition in oriental sense is neither transcendentalistic nor immanentistic; it is the nonseparation of transcendent being from immanent being. The non-duality of transcendence and immanence is to the orient not merely metaphysical speculation or aesthetical experience but an ontological-existential necessity.

That which is an existential necessity can only be attained existentially, that is by one who approaches it with all that he is and not simply as a philosopher or as an aesthete or as a moralist. That alone which transcends both the aesthetic and the theoretic, and which yet supports both the aesthetic and the theoretic, gives life, and that is what oriental spirituality points to.

The Japanese scholar, Hajime Nakamura, has presented an interpretation of oriental thought which takes issue with Northrop's. In his book, *Ways of Thinking of Eastern People,* Nakamura has tried to compare and contrast the ways of thinking of four Asiatic cultures by analyzing both the forms of linguistic expression and the general cultural patterns characterizing them. He does not relate these differences to underlying philosophies as Northrop tries to do, but studies them objectively as given in the respective cultures. His approach to oriental ways of thinking is thus in certain essential aspects directly opposed to Northrop's:

> There has long been a tendency to think in terms of a dichotomy between East and West, presupposing two mutually opposed cultural sets of values labeled "Occidental" and "Oriental." Thus the Oriental way of thinking is represented as "spiritual," "introverted," "synthetic," and "subjective," while the Occidental is represented as "materialistic," "extroverted," "analytic," and "objective." This sort of explanation by paired opposites is now rejected as too simple; the cultures of the "Orient" and "Occident" are too diversified and each one is extremely complex.[1]

[1]Hajime Nakamura, *Ways of Thinking of Eastern People* (Honolulu: East-West Center Press, 1964), p. 3.

Rejecting oversimplified renditions of oriental thought, he disputes the claim that oriental ways of thinking are illogical, and rather asserts that they are logical:

> The thought represented by Tertullian's aphorism, "credo quia absurdum," or "I believe because it is absurd," had no receptivity in India. The Indians are, at the same time, logical since they generally have a tendency to sublimate their thinking to the universal; they are at once logical and rationalistic. On the contrary, many religions of the West are irrational and illogical, and this is acknowledged by the Westerners themselves.[1]

> At first sight the Chinese give us the impression of being indifferent to logical exactitude. The ways of expression in the Chinese language are extremely ambiguous, and the historical fact that there has never been a development of formal logic (apart from the short lived Mohist school) among the Chinese seems to support this view. To be indifferent to rules of formal logic, however, is not necessarily to be irrational. It is widely known that Chinese thought, due to its rationalistic character, exerted a great influence upon the philosophy of enlightenment of the modern West.[2]

Nakamura repudiates the notion proclaimed by Northrop of a unified oriental culture:

> We must disavow the *cultural unity* of the West as we did in the case of the East.[3]

Instead, he sees four different major cultures in the Far East, all permeated by Buddhism, but each having absorbed Buddhism in its own distorted way:

> I intend to concentrate on India, China, Tibet, and Japan. My reason is that among these four peoples alone did there exist—however imperfectly—a study of traditional Buddhist logic, which came first from India to the other three areas, and then developed independently in each. I believe that the various other peoples of the East have nearly the same ways of thinking as one or another of these four. Specif-

[1]*Ibid.*, p. 17.
[2]*Ibid.*, p. 16.
[3]*Ibid.*, p. 24.

ically, one may say that Ceylon, Burma, Thailand, and Western Indo-China (Cambodia and Laos) are akin to India. Central Asia and Mongolia are akin to pre-communist Tibet. Manchuria, Korea and Eastern Indo-China (Vietnam) are akin to China. Thus, an examination of the ways of thinking of these four is, in effect, a study of the most influential peoples of the East. It is only after such a study, if at all, that a generalized view of the ways of thinking of Eastern peoples can emerge.[1]

Since Nakamura rejects the cultural unity of the orient, his methodology and standpoint are in one way pluralistic:

> We may offer, in the last analysis, the following hypothesis: There is no such thing as a single fundamental principle which determines the characteristic ways of thinking of a people. Various factors, as mentioned above, related in *manifold ways,* each exerting its influence, enter into the ways of thinking of a people. If we deal with the question of the existential basis which brings about differences of ways of thinking, we see no way left for us but to take the standpoint of pluralism.[2]

However, even while admitting that there is no one culture common to the whole of East Asia, he acknowledges a kind of relationship between the four different ways of thinking in the orient. Without reducing them to one pattern, he finds them all penetrated by a thread of universality, namely Buddhism. To Nakamura, true universality is not opposed to particularity. Rather, the fundamental meaning of universality is that it mysteriously relates itself to other particularities. In this way, Buddhism has taken root within each culture without displacing the particularity of the culture. Thus Nakamura de-particularizes Buddhism. He does not view it as one religion which opposes others but rather as something spiritual and essentially universal:

> Buddhism is not a special religion which conflicts with other religions, but is, in itself, the Absolute Truth.

[1]*Ibid.,* p. 4.
[2]*Ibid.,* p. 37.

> Heretics are nothing but an offshoot-manifestation of the ul-
> timate truth. From the absolute point of view there is in
> the universe only one principle called "Buddhism." . . . As
> a result, Buddhism, in spreading over the Asian countries,
> caused less friction among the indigenous faiths of the peo-
> ples who had received it. Native or traditional faiths and
> customs were scarcely destroyed by Buddhists and could
> easily survive; so long as they were seen as ethical from the
> Buddhist point of view, they were able to remain in exis-
> tence side by side with the newly-arrived Buddhism, and
> sometimes were absorbed in Buddhism. In later days Bud-
> dhism itself fused into one of the native religions, giving
> them philosophical foundations.[1]

Nakamura's interpretation of oriental cultures is evidently
far more subtle than Northrop's in that he endeavors to
hold both its universalistic and its particularistic dimension
in balance, and thus to avoid a simplistic universalism on
the one hand as well as a fragmented pluralism on the
other:

> Those who deny the cultural singleness of the East are
> prone to disavow the universality of Eastern thought. But
> logically speaking, it is inconsistent to deny the universality
> of Eastern thought as a consequence of disavowing the
> singleness of the East, dividing it into a numer of wholes,
> and at the same time recognizing a mutual (unilateral) in-
> fluence among these cultural wholes. We must avoid this in-
> consistency. We deny the singleness of the East but affirm
> the establishment of a number of cultural wholes. And it is
> because of this that we should like to acknowledge a *univer-
> sal significance* in certain aspects of various thought-sys-
> tems established in East Asia.[2]

For Nakamura, the thread upon which particular religions
in the orient are strung is the spirit of tolerance and conciliation. This spirit was intensified by Buddhism but was already an ingredient of oriental cultures or they would not
have been so readily open to Buddhism. The orient, according to Nakamura, is not exclusive but inclusive. Although

[1]*Ibid.*, p. 169.
[2]*Ibid.*, p. 28.

there are particular religions in the orient, they do not stand in direct opposition to each other. Neither Christianity nor Judaism nor Islam ever attained to such a harmony among themselves, each of them is in a way exclusive. And thus the history of the occident is full of religious antagonisms, anathema, and persecutions:

> Generally speaking, we *cannot find in any Indian religion the conception of "heretic"* in the sense of Western usage.[1]

> These religious attitudes differ from those in the West. In the history of Europe we often find religious antagonisms which inevitably led to political and military conflicts. But we can hardly find many cases of religious wars in India. There were, of course, in India a few rulers who adhered to some indigenous faith and oppressed some of the universal religions arising among the Indian people. But we cannot find any rulers who were Buddhists or Jainists and who persecuted other religions.[2]

> Religious wars or struggles over ideology, which frequently arose in Europe, did not arise in China. It is true that Buddhism was frequently suppressed, not because of Buddhist doctrine, but because the Buddhist organization menaced and weakened the nation's power politically and economically. While in Mohammedan countries fighting sometimes started on account of violations of such religious customs as eating pork, religious wars never arose in China.[3]

In this way, Nakamura is critical of occidental intolerance and disharmony. He does not see working there the kind of universality indigenous to the orient. To him, it is not true universality where religion is universalized by force. It is his idea that real universality cannot emanate from crusades, or excommunications. Universality to the orient is inseparable from the spirit of tolerance and harmony, and for Nakamura this is a lesson which the West has yet to learn:

[1]*Ibid.*, p. 170.
[2]*Ibid.*, p. 171.
[3]*Ibid.*, p. 285.

By reflecting upon the seemingly irrelevant ways of thinking of the East Asians, we can be *critical* of the philosophical thoughts of the West. And as result of the criticism,
we should be able to acquire an efficient base for going forward towards the establishment of a new and truly universal philosophy.[1]

While conceding Nakamura's point here, it needs also
to be said that he does not himself apprehend the fullest intention of the oriental sense of tolerance. He takes it as a
sociological or cultural given and seems unaware of its ontological roots. The orientation towards an absolute which
transcends opposites is universal in the orient, and the religious longing is directed towards it. *Therefore,* there is no
disposition to uphold or to fight for one approximation to
the absolute as against another. In short, it is a kind of
true awareness of the absolute which engenders the spirit
of tolerance as between differing approaches to the absolute. Because of this, Buddhism was able to penetrate
without *force* and its own universalistic emphasis intensified the spirit of conciliation and tolerance which had previously existed. Western peoples do seem more legalistic,
objectivistic and equate religion and truth with particular
systems. As a result, there have been endless conflicts between religions in the occident. Nakamura's positivistic
presentation sees the oriental attitude as an underground
fact, and as such it is no more praiseworthy than intolerance. In other words, oriental tolerance is ontologically
grounded tolerance and not solely a desideratum of the
moral consciousness. Nor can true tolerance result from
the exhortation to be tolerant. It is not sustainable by human decision and effort alone. Tolerance—when it is
tried—is intolerable, that is, forced, contrived, artificial.
Ontological tolerance, however, is that which is one with
man's whole being. What works in this kind of tolerance is
not an intellectual perception or a moral decision but the
presence of an absolute which is not in opposition to anything and which is not defined by exclusion.

[1]*Ibid.,* p. 32.

The Indian attitude towards religious pluralism, at its best, has also generally reflected the ancient Vedic dictum: "Truth is one; the sages call it by various names." In its deepest meaning it has been understood to signify both the universality of Truth itself and the impossibility of identifying it with any particular formulation. Hence the truth is not an objectivity identifiable as Hinduism. There are only various schoolings—suitable to different ages, climes and temperaments—for bringing man to the realization of the highest. But the highest is not to be equated with any school that educates for it. Reaching it is tantamount to a kind of graduation from schools.

However, in fact, the unity of truth has frequently been understood on a lower level, that is, more abstractly, as an essence which can be distilled and formulated. This manner of understanding is typified by Bhagavan Das who seeks the underlying unity of religions, East and West. In his book *The Essential Unity of All Religions,* he has endeavored to establish unity in place of plurality in the world, and to find it through world religion:

> (sic) Whole and sole purpose of this book is to endeavor to show a way to establish Concord in place of horrible Discord, which pervades (sic) world generally and India specially, by means of a rational World-Order based on and issuing out of a World-Religion.[1]

His concern is for humanity's practical needs and his proposal therefore has organizational dimensions as well as theoretical aspects:

> . . . that *best,* indeed, *only,* way of establishing peace and promoting general welfare throughout their respective dominions, and therefore India as a whole, is to teach and preach persistently, in every corner of the land, the *Common Essentials of All Religions,* and to establish, on (sic) basis of *scientific psychological principles,* included in that Universal World Religion, a Rational Socio-Individual Or-

[1]Bhagavan Das, *The Essential Unity of All Religions* (Bombay: Bharatiya Vidya Bhavan, 1960), p. xliii.

ganization, which will fulfill all just needs of all persons of
all creeds, castes, colours, races, and both sexes, *i.e.,* fill
all stomachs, cover all backs, provide roofs over all heads,
ensure decent family life, and bring livelihood-giving suitable work and appropriately qualified worker together.[1]

He insists on a universal solution to the human predicament, although each human existence is particular:

> Underneath, soaked through and through, permeating, per-
> vading, holding fast together, all Multitude, remains ever
> the Unity. This is the One Fact to be remembered always.[2]

To Das, the unity infusing in the multitude has to be
promoted by man's faith and action. To him, it is the essence of the unity that man should have a kind of common
faith in man's finitude and God's infinitude. Such a faith
seems necessary to him to hold men together. Proclaiming
such a faith is basic to the unity of the world religions, he
insists that faith is not enough unless implemented by
man's actions. Faith issuing in man's moral action can
unite anything which is separated:

> Conscious *conviction* that every 'finite' is created, ideated,
> maintained, 'held together,' and periodically manifested
> and in-drawn, by the Infinite; this, and corresponding *Phil-
> anthropic desire* and *action,* may be said to make up the
> whole of Religion. . . . For what else can 'hold together'
> living beings than mutual 'rightfulness' and 'du(e)-tiful-
> ness,' mutual righteousness and duteousness, mutual rights-
> and-duties, through common 'submission' to the will of the
> Divine Self?[3]

So faith and action for others are essential to religious
unity, and they basically function to hold mankind together:

> The one purpose of Religion (*legere,* to bind) is to bind the
> hearts of human beings to each other and to God.

[1]*Ibid.,* pp. xlvi-xlvii.
[2]*Ibid.,* p. 92.
[3]*Ibid.,* pp. 107-108.

Realization of Self in all as God in all, and consequent service of all as service of God, is (sic) perfection and completion of Religion.[1]

The nearest Indian word for religion is perhaps *dharma*.
According to Das, it literally means "holding or binding to-
gether" which is identical with the Latin word "legere."
Das quotes the *Mahabharata* to support this etymology:

That which binds fast all beings, each to each,
With bonds of rights-and-duties; binding these
Also together, in unfailing law
Of action and Reaction, whence arise
Reward for good and Punishment for ill,
And thus preserves mankind—Dharma is That.[2]

Sometimes, it is necessary to deny man's own self for the
sake of the unity of all mankind. And sometimes, it is also
necessary to deny a unity which is divorced from his own
personal integrity. To Das, the twofold denial is necessary
and requires an Archimedean point; and this is the sense of
relation between the divine (Self) and the human (self). To
Das, it is very important for man to know and feel that he
is a part of the divine. The true self or life is to affirm that
in oneself or in others which is a part of the divine and to
deny that in oneself or in others which is apart from the divine. Therefore, Das holds that man's sensing of the relationship between the human and the divine is the quintessence of religion:

The self-sacrifice of each *smaller* self for the sake of the
larger Self, which larger self is *felt* to be embodied in Society as a *whole;* and the corresponding self-sacrifice of
that *larger* Self or Society for the sake of each *smaller* self,
which smaller self is *felt* to be integral *part* of the
whole—this mutual self-sacrifice, though internally motivated by all-wise Philanthropic Love, has yet to be externally regulated by all-loving Wisdom; through Laws which
lay down rights-and-duties, which bind rights with duties,

[1]*Ibid.,* p. 759.
[2]*Ibid.,* p. 105.

and all human beings with the bonds of both. The *feeling,* and the implicit and explicit *recognition,* of the omni-presence of the large Self; and of one's particular smaller self being a part of, and subordinate to It, as a cell or a tissue in an organism; this feeling, this recognition, may be said to be the quintessence of 'religion' or 'religiousness.'[1]

The essential unity of all religions is constituted by the recognition of man's relationship with the divine.

For Das, man's relationship with the divine is finally his surrender to the divine. Man's will has to be replaced by the divine will:

> The word *Islām* has a profound and noble meaning which is, indeed, by itself, the very essence of religion. Derived from *salm,* peace, shānti, it means 'peaceful acceptance' of God; calm resignation, submission, surrender, pra-n i-dhāna, prapatti, of the small self to the Great Self; letting out of egoism and letting in of Universalism; namáskāra, na mama kintu ṭava īhā, "Thy will be done, Lord!, not mine"; whence only the mind, the heart, at peace with itself and with all the world.[2]

> The significance of 'Ḍharma' is the same; for what else can 'hold together' living beings than mutual 'rightfulness' and du(e)-ti-ful-ness,' mutual righteousness and duteousness, mutual rights-and-duties, through common 'submission' to the Will of the Divine Self?[3]

The will of the divine self has to be made known objectively, that is articulated as laws which are both good and wise. And good and wise laws will embody both a bill of rights and a bill of duties. A bill of rights without a bill of duties is irresponsible, while a bill of duties without a bill of rights is oppressive. Thus, the necessary balance between duty and right has to be made by good and wise legislators who fear God:

How may human beings ascertain what the Will of the Di-

[1]*Ibid.,* pp. 106-107.
[2]*Ibid.,* pp. 107-108.
[3]*Ibid.,* p. 108.

vine Self is, generally; and, even more, in particular cases. (sic) The answer, in brief, is: (a) Universal Essential Religion, Scientific Religion, Spiritual Science, tell us what that Will is, generally; (b) *particularly, good-and-wise* laws, defining rights-and-duties, made by *good-and-wise* legislators, who know love, fear God, *i.e.,* the Supreme, Universal Self of All; who therefore disinterestedly wish well to all just interests of all sections, classes, vocations; who, as far as is humanly possible, are 'near God,' are 'Sons of God,' are embodiments of the Higher, Better, Nobler, Wiser, Philanthropic Self of the People, and who are sincerely trusted, honoured, and duly selected and elected by the People to make laws;—such laws will represent the Divine Will, as nearly as possible for human beings.[1]

Man's conformity to objective laws is thus seen by Das necessary for mankind to come closer towards universal or the unity of all religions. Wherever man's will does not conform to these laws it is to be eliminated. In other words, personal will is not a part of the divine will; and thus it has to be separated from the divine will. For Das, this is the meaning of fearing God.

Moreover the divine will for mankind must be proclaimed and made manifest in a worldwide organization based on all mankind. Without such, the unity of mankind and of religion remains an unembodied idea prerequisite to the setting up of a universal organization and is a weakening of attachments to particular organizations, and thus in turn means seeing religions as but approximations to Religion:

It is to be hoped that before very long, with the help of that same completely unified science, it will soon come to be recognized that religions, too, are not many, but that Religion is one; and, finally, that Science and Religion are but different aspects of, or even only different names for, the same great body of Truth and its application which may be called the Science or Code of Life. If, formerly, every act was done in the name and under the guidance of religion, and laterly, has tended to be done in the name of science, there is reason to hope that, in (sic) future, it may be done in the name of Spiritual or Religious Science.[1]

Das, it would seem, takes Religion very seriously even as he takes religions rather lightly. He is therefore in perpetual peril of slighting time, place and history and of seeking salvation *in abstracto*:

> All this clearly signifies that Religion is necessary to man; that no *particular form* of religion is indispensable; that there are two alternatives open to us, either to reject all religions or to accept all religions; that both are impracticable; and that, therefore, the only practical, as also best, most satisfying, and wise course, is the third alternative, to sift out the elements of *Essential Religion* from the non-essential (though, for their time, place, and circumstances, useful) forms, of all the great religions extant, and feed the younger generation with those vital grains, instructing them that the husks are useful only for preserving and storing the grains in, and not for eating and assimilating.[2]

Das seems preoccupied with external universality, identity, similarity, rather than internal unity, identity, similarity and from this point of view, encounters two serious difficulties. First of all, he is concerned with the universal which is isolated from the particular. Second, he seeks for it externally. Lacking particular commitment to any religious tradition occidental or oriental, Das denies the necessity of a pluralism of religions. As a result, he neglects man's individuality, unique religious traditions, and particular religious histories. Das claims that the particular is less important than the universal:

> This whole attempt, to bring together parallel texts of several Scriptures, to prove identities and similarities, may, perhaps, fail to satisfy some critics, who would insist that minute differences should be at least as clearly brought out and emphasized as, if not more than, resemblances. They would, no doubt, be quite right, from their own standpoint, and for purposes of accurate intellectual scholarship.

---

[1]*Ibid.*, p. 19.
[2]*Ibid.*, pp. 71-72.

The compiler's plea is that "intellectual" interest is not the only interest of the book; that 'emotional' and 'practical' interests are of at least as great concern in it; that minute differences are already far too much stressed and acted on, to great harm of mankind; that resemblances are too much ignored, to their great loss; that even intellectually, what varies with each, deserves to be regarded as superficial, *Non*-Essential, and what runs through and is common to all, to be regarded as Core and Essence; and that, therefore, essential points, on which all religions agree, should be given far more prominence than they have been hiterto, and be regarded as (sic) very Heart of All Religions, as (sic) very Core of Truth; on the 'democratic principle' of (sic) 'majority vote'; and for the very important and truly practical purpose of promoting mutual Good Understanding and Peace all over Earth.[1]

Although Das frequently speaks of the importance of the particular, in fact, he deems the universal as prior to the particular. In this respect, Das is a kind of Platonist:

Let us recognise such differences, 'realities,' which constitute the 'personal' element or 'personality,' by all means; but let us regard them as of less importance, as changing, passing, therefore Non-Essential; and let us recognise more fully, 'idealities,' the 'impersonal' or 'all-personal' element, and regard them as of greater importance, persisting through changes, permanent, and therefore Essential.[2]

It (Particularity) too has an obvious and necessary place in the evolutionary Scheme of God's Nature, Universal Self's Nature. But we have to moderate it, reconcile it with, slowly transmute it into, its opposite; more and more. This is not impossible; rather, it too is equally ordained by that same Nature.[3]

Das's proposal can be expressed in the analogy of the man who tries to combine six blind men's descriptions of a living elephant, and to consider his description as being the living elephant. One of the blind men had caught the end

[1]*Ibid.*, pp. xxi-xxii.
[2]*Ibid.*, p. xxv.
[3]*Ibid.*, p. xxvi.

of the elephant's tail, and proclaimed the elephant is to be just like a broom. Another had felt the trunk, and declared that the elephant resembles a tree. A third found the abdomen, and said that it is just like a drum. A fourth touched an ear, and insisted that it is like a fan. A fifth grasped a leg, and described it as a column. The last felt the tusk, and said that the elephant is just like a spear. Each one of six blind men's claims describes one facet of the whole elephant. Knowing and observing this, Das tries to combine the claims of six blind men, and hopes that he can synthesize them all without contradiction. This method is obviously confronted not without its difficulties.

First, he would seem to be too presuming to those who hold their own faith firmly and who would resist his effort to wipe out their particular attachments. And secondly, his attempt to make the universal out of the particular religions is in itself a particular project. Although his project is allegedly based on "well-planned religious instructions for the universal brotherhood," he is in fact like the man who tries to combine six blind men's claims and to consider his synthesis as an elephant. At best his synthesis is a pictured-elephant—at worst it is a dead elephant. The unity he achieves is contrived by abstraction and possesses no living inwardness of its own. It is not based on anything but abstract ideas and it can have no dynamic unless it can be concretized. It is not organically rooted in the soil of anyone's life, and the *divine* to which we are to surrender is only an abstract idea with no content, to which one can give perhaps intellectual assent but no whole-hearted allegiance. Thus it cannot be found in searching for parallel texts in the several Scriptures, but with the confronting of one's own life in its utmost inwardness. Any answer to the problem of universal and particular is abstract when it is achieved externally. Intellectually viewed, unity or essence is always set over against disunity or existence. As a result, those who approach the problem of the universal and the particular externally either lean towards disunity or human existence or are champions of unity or essence. But the religious approach towards the same problem is both existential and ontological. In other words, the religious problem is not to search for the universal outside of man's own self but to *be* universal as particular. In such an ontological relatedness or non-duality of the universal and the particular, the universal is the particular.

Das identifies a pictured-elephant with a particular living elephant. Life itself cannot be grasped and organized outside of a man's own life. Nor can it be abstracted from the plurality of lives, because it will be a corpse as soon as it is without a particular life of its own; ignoring man's own existence, Das cannot really create anything religious.

The attempt to go beyond particular religions by extracting a common essence can never make contact with anything living. Let us then turn from the inspection of religious traditions to man himself. Is it possible that man houses the universal within itself?

Allan Watts would not only answer this question in the affirmative, but would add that it is the distinctive significance of oriental spirituality that it recognizes this. In his *Supreme Identity,* he tries to discover the universal Self in the particular self. His proposal in principle is more inwardly directed than Bhagavan Das'. And he has no sympathy for the attempt to reach truth by eclectic mergers:

> The wisdom which Asia has to offer embodies not only the human mind's most profound understanding of life, but also a knowledge essential to human order and sanity. In some of my former works, notably *Behold the Spirit,* I have tried to show how this wisdom might, as it were, be woven into the fabric of Christianity. I have come to see, however, that such interweaving is unsatisfactory, for 'no man putteth new cloth into old garments.' Christianity needs no additions or amplifications from outside, and the attempt to incorporate any oriental doctrine within it, as if the two kinds of doctrine were of the same order, is merely confusing. It is like trying to interpolate fragments of a symphony into the midst of a dance. Properly, the two

should be set side by side, and related by analogy instead of mixture.[1]

To Watts, oriental religious ideas are in the final analysis not religious but super-religious:

> For there is a realm of spiritual wisdom which religion as we know it can express by analogy only. When we try to speak of it more directly, we must go beyond religious language, beyond the forms of thought which dogma, sacrament and theology can legitimately employ. It is a wisdom which neither conflicts with nor supersedes religion, because it is in some sense outside the religious sphere. Its province is a mystery with which religion, as such, is not *directly* concerned, and about which it has no official teaching, since it cannot be expressed directly in the religious type of language. But though it lies beyond the religious sphere, religion interprets it as a dancer interprets music. This is, however, a music to which we are very largely deaf, for which reason most of us must rely on religion for the only connection with it which, in this life, we can live. Yet if the dance of religion is to proceed with spirit and strength, at least the leaders of the dance must hear the tune.
>
> In itself this wisdom has a glory which absolutely defies description.[2]

Watts sees clearly that oriental spiritual wisdom goes beyond anything which can be communicated by words. However that which cannot be expressed in words does not totally transcend from human being, but is hidden in human consciousness. Thus, to search for that which is beyond description is not to search for it abstractly but concretely:

> It tries to express that inner depth of consciousness which is not accessible to thought and feeling because it lies behind them.[3]

[1]Alan Watts, *The Supreme Identity* (London: Faber & Faber Ltd., no year given), p. 12.
[2]*Ibid.,* p. 13.
[3]*Ibid.,* p. 13.

Oriental wisdom is related to man's ultimate inwardness and hence defies descriptions by language designed for objective references. Conventional religious language no longer convinces the modern sophisticated occidental consciousness because its language is incredible. Oriental wisdom is, however, immune to the critique made by linguistic analysis. Watts sees this wisdom not as yet another religion, but as metaphysics in the following sense of the term.

> Modern philosophy, science, and even religion seem to have lost hope and, all too often, interest itself in the possibility of metaphysical knowledge. By knowledge of this kind we mean neither religious belief, philosophical speculation, nor scientific theory. We mean actual experience or immediate realization of that ultimate Reality which is the ground and cause of the universe, and thus the principle and meaning of human life.[1]

> We must follow Guénon in using the word "metaphysic" for this order of knowledge, despite the fact that in modern philosophy as well as in certain religious cults of to-day it means something quite different. Aristotle is supposed to have given the title *Metaphysics* to one of his treatises just because it was written after the *Physics,* but it would be more reasonable to think that the word properly refers to the knowledge of that which is beyond ($\mu\epsilon\tau\alpha'$) the natural order ($\phi\upsilon\acute{o}\iota\varsigma$)—that is to the universal, infinite, and eternal, as distinct from and beyond the individual, the finite and the temporal.[2]

Thus metaphysics is not for Watts a purely speculative enterprise which goes beyond all experiences, but is instead the experiential realization of the universal Self within each particular self. To him, that ultimate which is within is far more important than the particular itself. His approach abstracts from all concern with the concrete history of religions. Watts approaches oriental religions metaphysically rather than historically. And for him it is essential to under-

[1] *Ibid.,* p. 18.
[2] *Ibid.,* p. 32.

stand the reason why the universal Self is to be separated from the particular selves:

> It must be understood, then, that the Self, the *atma* which is *Brahma,* is not to be confused with the empirical ego, with the soul-body wherewith the conscious Self is normally identified. Furthermore the infinite Reality which constitutes the Self is not, save by analogy, the external, positively described space-time God of Religion. The Principle *tat tvam asi* does *not* imply the consequence, 'Hence I, John Smith, am God Almighty!'[1]

Thus, he does not see oriental spirituality as resting on any concrete basis, and he is interested in the oriental mentality or spirit and not in oriental peoples. Man's relation to the universal spirit is central, and all particular relationships between man and man seem for Watts to be secondary. Watts speaks as a philosopher and is perhaps unwittingly arrogant towards the merely human:

> Man is by nature a philosopher, and cannot be otherwise.[2]

To be a philosopher is taken to mean that there must be a common end to which all men must agree philosophically, and that end is to realize the ultimate reality which is within. Not to agree with this is to agree not to have a common human bond:

> To agree to differ, to let everyone follow quite independent or contradictory views of man's end, is merely to agree *not* to have any true social union, and to let our society disintegrate spiritually as it is in fact now doing. To agree that we must all eat, drink, and live at peace is still not to agree about ends, about any significant principle of unity. To agree not to philosophize at all, which is the only way to have unity on the purely animal level, is quite impossible since a decision is already the philosophical opinion of agnosticism.[3]

[1]*Ibid.,* p. 84.
[2]*Ibid.,* p. 20.
[3]*Ibid.,* p. 20.

In short, individualism and pluralism are insufficient to attain human common unity. It is individualism that one goes one's own way without hurting others, but this does not engender basic human relations. It is pluralism that there is no one unifying principle by which everything is viewed, but this gives no basis for collective life. In other words, Watts tries to propose a universal end which all men can agree to realize and in which they shall be united. To him, man is not for his particular existence but for the universal end. Individualists as well as pluralists are really obstructionists impeding the realization of human unity. To him, those who search for the universal end are not anti-social escapists. On the contrary:

> But it should be obvious by now that the real escapist, the
> real obscurantist who balks the realization of social unity,
> is precisely the person who will not face the question of
> man's true end.[1]

On the philosophical level, Watts' conception of the relation of the universal and the particular is not without merit. Its adequacy in relation to oriental religiosity is another matter:

> For the moment it will be enough to remember that the
> two are 'other' without being 'opposed,' somewhat as
> shape is other than colour but not at all incompatible with
> it, though this is by no means a perfect analogy. In truth
> the universal and infinite has no opposite at all because it is
> absolutely all-inclusive.[2]

Watts tries to transcend the "opposing dualism." He sees the universal as not merely up-there but within human beings. His task is not to find the universal from the outside but to see it within himself. And thus, he does not reject his own particular position as a philosopher and his own individuality as a man. Nevertheless, on his terms, the relationship between the particular and the universal is still du-

[1]*Ibid.*, p. 25.
[2]*Ibid.*, p. 33.

alistic in the sense that relationship by definition occurs between the two which are thus given a kind of separated existence. He does not grant to the particular any ontological
relevance in relation to the universal. Salvation comes from
the universal alone. Man's search for the universal cannot
be fulfilled by his own faculties. One can almost detect a
Calvinistic aroma in the following:

> The realization of metaphysical knowledge will therefore
> depend on the presence in man of some higher faculty than
> reason or feeling.[1]

> That this realization is the work of God and not of man, of
> the Self and not of ego, is the reason why 'Thy will be
> done' is no resolution but a prayer.[2]

Thus for Watts, the bridge between the particular and the
universal must be built by the universal. His interpretation
cannot finally claim to embody a non-duality of the universal and the particular. Watts, in fact, calls his view a "dualism of transcendence" as distinguished from that of opposition. This dualism of transcendence is described in the
following statements:

> Because the infinite is *not opposed* to the finite, being all-in-
> clusive, there is no real problem of creation, i.e., of *how* it
> is possible for the infinite to produce the finite. The infinite
> includes the possibility of the finite world in principle and
> by definition. It produces things by becoming finite, with-
> out ceasing to be its infinite Self. Yet it is not the One as
> opposed to the Many, but includes both unity and multiplic-
> ity. . . . But the infinite *includes* the finite in a unity (or
> non-duality) which does not obliterate distinctions.[3]

> A realization of eternity does not involve any leaving of the
> finite *behind,* because from the eternal standpoint all time
> is present. There can thus be no idea of passing out of the
> finite into the infinite in the order of temporal succession.
> A *nirvana* in which finite existence belonged solely to the

---

[1]*Ibid.*, pp. 33-34.
[2]*Ibid.*, p. 191.
[3]*Ibid.*, p. 45.

past would not be a true realization at all, but, on the contrary, a strictly temporal state.[1]

Because the infinite transcends all dualism, it is able to include dualism, so that realization is in no way incompatible with everyday awareness of the objective world, with physical life and activity. The profound detachment of the Self from the ego and the world is not a detachment of rejection but of acceptance and love. True detachment from things consists in letting them be free to be themselves, which is to say, in not confusing them with the Self. They are confused with the Self when identified with it unconsciously, and when separated from it as if it were an object like themselves. To seek God or the Self as an object of knowledge is to deny the transcendence of the infinite by putting it in the class of objects.[2]

Though it is not lacking in philosophical subtlety, this does not touch the central core of oriental religiosity. To the orient, religiosity is not grounded on any dualism whatsoever. It is still dualistic to state that the universal is not opposed to the particular. In other words, man's search for the universal is not a search either within or without. Where *within* is set over against without, a dualism has been contrived, and how is the absolute to be domiciled in one place rather than another.

The search for the truly universal is a search for man's whole particularity without remainder. The search for it is not based on forgetfulness of man's particular existence. In other words, the universal as the ultimate goal of life in oriental thought is no other than man's true wholeness. Thus the universal is to the orient not an abstraction but concrete itself. Truth comes neither from outside nor from inside, but from man's concrete life. It cannot be real if the universal imposes itself upon the particular. Anything—that is religiously true—rings true only if the universal is not set over against the particular. In the oneness of a particular seeker and a universal sought, there is neither trying, desiring, nor doing. Man can be filled with truth itself, reality

[1]*Ibid.*, p. 71.
[2]*Ibid.*, p. 187.

itself, being itself, or ultimacy only when man's activity ceases to stand in opposition to his whole being. Watts understands this in his way but, in the end, the process is reduced to a kind of clever game:

> The Self will not let us do nothing. As soon as we begin to desire realization, this is the sign that the progress has begun. Our search for the Self is moved by the Self. To become, or realize, what we are, we must first *try* to become it, in order to realize effectively that it is not necessary to do so (sic).[1]

Watts' problem here is that he presumes to be privy to the trade secrets of the absolute. If so, he is violating cosmic copyright laws in revealing them to all and sundry. The truth of the matter is that the whole thing is beyond cleverness and verbal solutions. The relation of the infinite to the finite, of the Self to the self and of the universal to the particular is to be encountered in realization. And it is not given to explication. Again, Watts' error is his overemphasis on the universal. Man's cosmic self is creatively both universal and particular. Identifying ultimacy with the universal side of self, Watts ignores the fact that the particular, the immediate, the ego, the small self or the human is no less significant than the universal Self. In other words, the existential fact that every man has his unique individuality has been treated harshly. Man's particularity can never fully yield itself to the ultimate goal of universality in abstraction. Man's need can be fulfilled neither by the surrender to immediacy nor by the pursuit of ultimacy alone, but through a wholeness in which ultimacy and immediacy are one. If this is true, man's task—as the orient thinks of it—is to simultaneously fulfill his immediate and particular needs but also to fulfill his ultimate and universal need. He has to realize the one without rejecting the other. Contrary to Tillich and to the whole Platonizing tradition, religion is not just ultimate concern but ultimate and immediate con-

[1]*Ibid.*, p. 165.

cern. Or we may say, for the orient, that alone is truly ultimate which is not set over against any immediate. To the
orient, the non-duality of these opposites is not only a
theory, but an actuality capable of realization.

Fung Yu-lan is an interesting and eminent Chinese
scholar whose interpretations of Chinese thought are
deeply influenced by occidental naturalism and humanism
to such an extent that he bypasses the religious inwardness of oriental thought. In *A Short History of Chinese Philosophy,* Fung states that Chinese ethics is devoid of religion:

> To the Westerner, who sees that the life of the Chinese peo-
> ple is permeated with Confucianism, it appears that Confu-
> cianism is a religion. As a matter of fact, however, Confu-
> cianism is no more a religion than, say, Platonism or
> Aristotelianism.[1]

Fung seeks to get beneath religion to the basic structure on
which the superstructure is erected. Fung calls the fundamental structure of Chinese traditions "Philosophy." To
Fung, religion is part of the superstructure. And thus it is
to him not fundamentally significant. He sees philosophy
as superior to religion and as closer to the universal:

> Every great religion *is* a philosophy with a certain amount
> of superstructure, which consists of superstitions, dogmas,
> rituals, and institutions. This is what I call religion.[2]

And more emphatically Fung says of the Chinese:

> They have not had much concern with religion because
> they have had so much concern with philosophy. They are
> not religious because they are philosophical. In philosophy
> they satisfy their craving for what is beyond the present ac-
> tual world. In philosophy also they have the super-moral
> values expressed and appreciated, and in living according
> to philosophy these super-moral values are experienced.[3]

[1]Fung Yu-lan, *A Short History of Chinese Philosophy* (New York: The Macmillan Company, 1948), p. 1.
[2]*Ibid.,* p. 3.
[3]*Ibid.,* pp. 4-5.

Thus it is clear that what is essential to Fung Yu-lan is not the religious but the philosophical. The universal is a product of systematic reflection on man's life. In other words, the universal is abstracted from man's living life itself. In this sense, the universal as understood by Fung is an idea and not a reality. By the same token, his philosophy is not a lived one but an abstracted one:

> For my part, what I call philosophy is systematic, reflective thinking on life. Every man, who has not yet died, is in life. But there are not many who think reflectively on life, and still fewer whose reflective thinking is systematic. A philosopher *must* philosophize; that is to say, he must think reflectively on life, and then express his thoughts systematically.[1]

In other words, a philosopher is to deal with theories, but not with life itself. He deals with objective knowledge, but not with wisdom, and he deals with the concept of the universe defined as "that which has nothing beyond," and not with the actual world.

On the other hand, Fung is true to the Chinese tradition in asserting that the function of philosophy in the Chinese sense of the word is not simply the collection of information but the sublimation of the mind. To illustrate, Fung quotes from the *Tao Te Ching:* "To work on learning is to increase day by day; to work on *Tao* (the Way, the Truth) is to decrease day by day." He has only a partial grasp of its meaning:

> The purpose of the former is what I call the increase of positive knowledge, that of the latter is the elevation of the mind. Philosophy belongs in the latter category.[2]

According to Fung, the elevation of the mind is the ultimate goal of human life and such an elevation of the mind cannot be achieved by any form of religion, but it can be attained by philosophy:

[1]*Ibid.,* p. 2.
[2]*Ibid.,* p. 5.

In the world of the future, man will have philosophy in the place of religion. This is consistent with Chinese tradition. It is not necessary that man should be religious, but it *is* necessary that he should be philosophical. When he is philosophical, he has the very best of the blessings of religion.[1]

To Fung, the elevation of mind is not merely idealistic but also realistic:

So far as the main tenet of its tradition is concerned, if we understand aright, it cannot be said to be wholly this-worldly, just as, of course, it cannot be said to be wholly other-worldly. It is both of this world *and* of the other world.[2]

The task of Chinese philosophy is to accomplish a synthesis out of these antitheses. That does not mean that they are to be abolished. They are still there, but they have been made into a synthetic whole. How can this be done? This is the problem which Chinese philosophy attempts to solve.[3]

His answer to the question, "How can this be done?" is to be a sage:

According to Chinese philosophy, the man who accomplishes this synthesis, not only in theory but also in deed, is the sage.[4]

According to Fung, a sage is described as being both this-worldly and other-worldly. His this-worldliness is his concern with the real world, and his other-worldiness means his sensitivity to the ideal world:

This-worldliness and other-worldliness stand in contrast to each other as do realism and idealism. The task of Chinese philosophy is to accomplish a synthesis out of these antitheses.[5]

Since the character of the sage, according to Chinese tradi-

[1] *Ibid.*, p. 6.
[2] *Ibid.*, pp. 7-8.
[3] *Ibid.*, p. 8.
[4] *Ibid.*, p. 8.
[5] *Ibid.*, p. 8.

tion, is one of sageliness within and kingliness without, the task of philosophy is to enable man to develop this kind of character. Therefore, what philosophy discusses is what the Chinese philosophers describe as the *Tao* (Way, or basic principles) of sageliness within and kingliness without.[1]

Since the subject matter of philosophy is the *Tao* of sageliness within and kingliness without, the study of philosophy is not simply an attempt to acquire this kind of knowledge, but is also an attempt to develop this kind of character. Philosophy is not simply something to be *known,* but is also something to be *experienced*.[2]

The purpose of the study of philosophy is to enable a man, *as a man,* to be a man, not some particular kind of man. Other studies—not the study of philosophy—enable a man to be some special kind of man.[3]

Thus Fung tries to identify a sage with a philosopher, and to say that Chinese philosophy enables man to develop such sagehood.

But the question needs to be asked: How does the sage achieve in his life that *coincidentia oppositorum* which intellectual reflection has never been able to accomplish in the whole history of human philosophical endeavor? The sage unites heaven and earth, the infinite and the finite, the ideal and the real, the ultimate and the immediate, the eternal and the temporal, intellect and feeling—all in his own being. No philosopher qua philosopher has this accomplishment to his credit. Religion claims the realization of it is possible, and necessary, and sagehood is the outcome of religious realization and not of philosophical reflection alone as Fung would have it.

Moreover, Fung misses another aspect of the Chinese tradition, and that is being-natural. To Fung, manhood is exclusively cultural, humanistic, volitional, and rational. In other words, Fung neglects the significance of being nat-

[1] *Ibid.,* p. 8.
[2] *Ibid.,* p. 10.
[3] *Ibid.,* p. 11.

ural, that is to say, he is insensitive to the religious ingredient of grace in the make-up of a sage. To Fung, sagehood is not the result of being natural, it comes from spiritual cultivation: "That is to say, in his sageliness, he accomplishes spiritual cultivation."[1] A sage or philosopher is one who shapes or polishes or cultures both his mind and society. The more one cultivates oneself and society, the more he becomes wise and his society becomes good. To Fung, the uncultivated is the undesirable. In other words, doing—spiritual and physical—is the essential in Fung's understanding of Chinese traditions. According to him, a philosopher is not primarily a thinker but also a doer. And rather his prime task as a philosopher is to forget thinking:

> In order to be one with the Great One, the sage has to transcend and forget the distinctions between things. The way to do this is to discard knowledge, and is the method used by the Taosits for achieving "sageliness within." The task of knowledge in the ordinary sense is to make distinctions; to know a thing is to know the difference between it and other things. Therefore to discard knowledge means to forget these distinctions.[2]

Naturalness, however, cannot be attained or realized by merely trying to discard or forget knowledge. Naturalness as this study conceives of it, is not in opposition to doing or knowing. The real meaning of naturalness is that both doing and knowing are in harmony with being natural. The human, whether in doing or knowing, does not stand in opposition to the natural. It is the central meaning of naturalness that the human in being natural does not impose itself upon anything. There is no naturalness, spontaneity or harmony, whenever there is opposition between beings. Confucius said that he reached the stage where he could do whatever his heart desired. In naturalness, morality does not suppress emotion or passion, nor does philosophy stand over against religion. In other words, naturalness comes into being only when there is existential harmony between

[1]*Ibid.*, p. 8.
[2]*Ibid.*, p. 115.

the opposites. In this sense, the natural is not merely the in-
stinctual or the material but also the existential or the ontological. Naturalness in the truest sense is man's whole
being acting unimpededly:

> Therefore, the sage manages affairs without doing any-
> thing, and conveys his instructions without the use of
> speech.[1]

> All things spring up, and there is not one which declines to
> show itself; they grow, and there is no claim made for their
> ownership; they go through their processes, and there is no
> expectation (of a reward for the results). The work is ac-
> complished, and there is no resting in it (as an achieve-
> ment).
> The work is done, but how no one can see; 'Tis this that
> makes the power not cease to be.[2]

> "The Man of Tao does not become distinguished; the
> greatest virtue is unsuccessful; the Great Man has no
> thought of self;" . . .[3]

Thus it appears that Fung has missed an essential dimension of sageliness, that is, its simultaneous embodiment of
the non-duality of the human and the natural.

In summary, then, it seems clear that in such modern
interpretations of oriental religiosity as we have examined
in this chapter there is evidenced a deficient awareness of
what we regard as its inmost intent. These interpretations
are in various degrees dualistic and represent attempts—largely intellectual and external—to grasp and present oriental religious culture as a body to objectivities.
Consequently they do not adequately communicate what
we have maintained as its focal awareness which is that of
life unfissured by dichotomies. For the orient, as we would
maintain, absolute life does not reside in a position, for
this will always engender an opposition. Absoluteness is all-
embracing, not exclusivistic. How to enter into a mode of
life which is holistic and unplagued by opposition is the ulti-

[1]*The Texts of Taoism*, Ch. 2.3., p. 96.
[2]*Ibid.*, Ch. 2. 3., p. 96.
[3]Chuang-Tzu, Ch. 17. 3., p. 427.

mate existential problem of oriental spirituality. Both the problem and its solution are bypassed by thinking along dualistic lines.

CHAPTER III

HINDUISM IN PERSEPCTIVE

Albert Schweitzer's interpretation of Indian thought is an interesting and influential example of an occidental attempt to understand Indian religious ideas. His treatment of Indian religious traditions is set forth in two books: *Christianity and the Religions of the World* and *Indian Thought and Its Development*. Schweitzer's object in dealing with Indian thought and the other religions has never been merely to satisfy theoretical curiosity:

> You and I are concerned with preaching the Gospel of Jesus in the world. We need to have a clear conception of the reasons why this gospel is for the highest wisdom. Why do we consider it to be the leaven which is to leaven the thought, the will and the hope of all mankind.[1]

To him, his own religion is superior to any other religion, simply because it is an ethical teaching:

> Christianity must, clearly and definitely, put before men the necessity of a choice betwen logical religion and ethical religion, and it must insist on the fact that the ethical is the highest type of spirituality, and that it alone is living spirituality.[2]

Schweitzer seems determined to defend his own Christianity in the light of the ethical criterion which he had worked out before undertaking the task of defense. Oriental reli-

[1] Albert Schweitzer, *Christianity and the Religions of the World* (New York: Doubleday, 1923), p. 19.

[2] *Ibid.*, p. 91.

gions are to him non-ethical religion; and as he came to this understanding his earlier sympathy for Indian religion abated.

From his youth, Schweitzer had been concerned with religious quest which in his mind took the formulation: How can the finite attain to the union with the infinite?

> Religion, I said, is the search for a solution of the problem how man can be in God and in the world at one and the same time.[1]

In his quest for an answer, Schweitzer was greatly influenced by Indian thought:

> Indian thought has greatly attracted me since in my youth I first became acquainted with it through reading the works of Arthur Schopenhauer. From the very beginning I was convinced that all thought is really concerned with the great problem of how man can attain to spiritual union with infinite Being. My attention was drawn to Indian thought because it is busied with this problem and because by its nature it is mysticism. What I liked about it also was that Indian ethics are concerned with the behaviour of men to all living beings and not merely with his attitude to his fellow-man and to human society.[2]

His understanding of Indian religious ideas was undoubtedly at this time somewhat influenced by his own religious questing, but in his later life, this approach came to be increasingly influenced by his own commitment to Christianity.

After he had decided to devote his life to helping Africans, he came to ask himself the reason for helping them. Without any rationale for helping others, a life for others seemed to him to be meaningless. For this reason, he struggled to "find the elementary and universal conception of the ethical which I had not discovered in any philos-

---

[1]*Ibid.*, p. 76.

[2]Albert Schweitzer, *Indian Thought and Its Development* (Boston: The Beacon Press, 1956), p. vi.

ophy."[1] While making his way through the African jungle, one day he found the ground for helping others: "Reverence for life." In the concept "reverence for life," his affirmation of life in this world had taken its root. "Now I knew," wrote Schweitzer, "that the world-view of ethical world and life-affirmation, together with its ideals of civilization is founded in thought."[2] His idea of reverence for life, therefore, was his whole rationalization for helping others.

His new concept "reverence for life" seemed to him to go contrary to his earlier interest in Indian thought. It also seemed to necessitate a rejection of Schopenhauer's claim that the Indian religious idea is superior to Christian idea. For Schopenhauer, both Christianity and Hinduism are rooted in the denial of the world and life. According to Schopenhauer, it is logically inevitable for any religion to be life-denying, simply because the spiritual life in its nature is unable to exist together with the material life, and thus the spiritual is directly opposed to the material. This entails the conclusion that man's salvation is to come from man's freedom from the material world. It is Schopenhauer's claim that negation of life in this world is the prerequisite of redemption and as such is the essence of Indian thought. Schweitzer sees his own concept of reverence for life as directly opposed to Schopenhauer's view.

Reverence for life being established as the foundation of his thought, Schweitzer then attempts to put it into practice in every area of his life and to base his moral evaluations upon it. From this point of view, the human situation is defined as follows:

> The most immediate fact of man's consciousness is the assertion: "I am life which wills to live, in the midst of life which wills to live," and it is as will-to-live in the midst-of-will-to-live that man conceives himself during every mo-

[1]Schweitzer, *Out of My Life and Thought* (New York: Henry Holt and Company, 1933), p. 185.
[2]*Ibid.*, pp. 185-186.

ment that he spends in meditating on himself and the world around him.[1]

According to Schweitzer, this is the context which calls for an ethical relationship of self and will-to-live and for an affirmation of his will-to-live:

> If man affirms his will-to-live, he acts naturally and honestly. He confirms an act which has already been accomplished in his instinctive thought by repeating it in his conscious thought. The beginning of thought, a beginning which continually repeats itself, is that man does not simply accept his existence as something given, but experiences it as something unfathomably mysterious. Life-affirmation is the spiritual act in which he ceases to live unreflectively and begins to devote himself to his life with reverence, in order to raise it to its true value. To affirm life is to deepen, to make more inward, and to exalt the will-to-live.[2]

His reverence for life or life-affirmation is to him a product of his experience of an ethical God:

> My life is completely and unmistakably determined by the mysterious experience of God revealing Himself within me as ethical Will and desiring to take hold of my life.[3]

For Schweitzer, that which is directly opposed to such an ethical element in life is pessimistic and undesirable. And thus he interprets Indian religious ideas as opposed to ethics:

> Man has now to decide what his relation to his will-to-live shall be. He can deny it. But if he bids his will-to-live change into will-not-to-live, as is done in Indian and indeed in all pessimistic thought, he involves himself in self-contradiction. He raises to the position of his world and life view something unnatural, something which is in itself untrue, and which cannot be carried to completion. Indian

[1] *Ibid.*, p. 186.
[2] *Ibid.*, p. 187.
[3] Schweitzer, *Christianity and the Religions of the World*, p. 84.

> thought, and Schopenhauer's also, is full of inconsistencies because it cannot help making concessions time after time to the will-to-live which persists in spite of all world and life denial, though it will not admit that the concessions are really such. Negation of the will-to-live is self-consistent only if it is really willing actually to put an end to physical existence.[1]

Negating non-ethical religious thought, Schweitzer claims that the ethical is the criterion employed for evaluating the essential substance of a religion. Any religion which is not mysteriously ethical is to him insignificant. To him, ethical mysticism is a highest form of religion:

> It is the ethical content, however, that determines its inner nature. The great question, therefore, which each religion must be asked is, how far it produces permanent and profound incentives to the inward perfecting of personality and to ethical activity.[2]
>
> The God whom we have within us as an ideal is an ethical personality.[3]

In other words, a religion can be real, only insofar as it is ethically mystical.

Consequently, Hindu religious ideas are to him deficient in this regard, although he believed that later Indian thought attempts to compensate for the indifference to ethics which he finds characteristic of the religion in its classical period.

But Schweitzer seems to overlook the fact that Hinduism is not so much one thing to be historically developed, as it is a many-splendored thing exhibiting simultaneously many levels. As it has been pointed out, Hinduism is not something which can be identified with an objective teaching or doctrine. Hinduism has no founder and no central authority, and thus it has no mandated context. Nevertheless, it accommodates itself to every level of human life. It adapts itself to an intellectual mind; it can also be fitted to

---

[1]Schweitzer, *Out of My Life and Thought,* p. 187.
[2]Schweitzer, *Christianity and the Religions of the World,* pp. 40-41.
[3]*Ibid.,* p. 40.

emotional as well as activistic temperaments. The many-ness of Hinduism is for the fitness of each individuality as well as for inner self. To fit into all human types and modes for the sake of helping all is the ultimate concern of Hindu religiosity. This fitness is called *Adhikara* and means that Hinduism has an intrinsic flexibility which enables it to become all things to all men.

Since Hinduism is not a package of ideas or doctrines, it is not an -ism. In reality there is no single thing to be called Hinduism. The word "Hinduism" in fact is an occidental word:

> The term 'Hinduism' is, in my judgment, a particularly false conceptualization, one that is conspicuously incompatible with any adequate understanding of the religious outlook of Hindus. Even the term 'Hindus' was unknown to the classical Hindus. 'Hinduism' as a concept certainly they did not have.[1]

The fundamental character of Hinduism is cosmic rather than historical. The Indo-Aryans call their own religion the Aryan Way (*ārya-dharma*) or the noble way. It was not seen as doctrine or teaching or idea of religion but as the way to cosmic life, and the way of cosmic life is also termed *sanātana dharma* (literally, the eternal way). Therefore, it cannot be subjected to history.

Hindu religious ideas, according to Schweitzer, are less ethical than Christian religious ideas, simply because Hindu mysticism emphasizes ecstasy in isolation from life in this world:

> . . . the real belief of the Brahmans is that man does not attain to union with the Brahman by means of any achievement of his natural power of gaining knowledge, but solely by quitting the world of the senses in a state of ecstasy and thus learning the reality of pure being.[2]

---

[1]Wilfred Cantwell Smith, *The Meaning and End of Religion* (New York: The Macmillan Company, 1963), p. 63.

[2]Schweitzer, *Indian Thought and Its Development*, p. 38.

Thus, Schweitzer views Hinduism as focusing on a kind of trance which is highly irrelevant to ordinary lives as well as to man's reason:

> And distinguishing Indian world-view from ours, there is yet another difference, which lies just as deep as that between world and life affirmation and world and life denial. That of India is monistic and mystical, ours is dualistic and doctrinaire.[1]

> When one first makes acquaintance with Indian thought, with what perplexity one faces the appearances alongside the Brahmanic doctrine of the Sāṃkhya doctrine, Jainism and Buddhism! Trivialities apart, they stand for the same world and life negation as does Brahminism.[2]

To Schweitzer, Indian mysticism holds that the infinite Being or *brahman* is identical with man's inner reality. The union to be achieved with *brahman* is to him clearly a special experience of an immaterial sort; an experience which excludes ordinary experiences:

> This consciousness of being uplifted above the world which is experienced in ecstasy is the condition determining Indian world and life negation.[3]

Schweitzer's view embodies a fallacious understanding of the matter which is very widely prevalent, namely, that mystical ecstasy is a purely psychological experience which calls for an obliteration of the world and the individual's personality. Where the supreme is viewed as in dualistic confrontation with the finite, to experience it necessitates a turning away from the finite. This understanding of the relationship of the finite and the infinite is to be found within Hinduism, as it is to be found in Christianity and in other religions. It sets up an ultimately competitive relation between the finite and the infinite, between the worldly and the unworldly and bids the seeker choose between them.

[1]*Ibid.*, p. 10.
[2]*Ibid.*, p. 65.
[3]*Ibid.*, p. 22.

This is not the final or highest understanding of the matter in Hinduism, however, since Hinduism seeks a One which is without a second and such a One does not require the setting aside of the second or third or fourth. Brahman is the reality of the world, not a reality in competition with the world. Were the latter the case, Schweitzer's indictment of Hinduism would be irrefutable. The attainment of *brahman* would then require the negation of this world. But Schweitzer has not understood the ultimately non-dualistic character of Hinduism even as he has avoided dealing with the unworldly aspect of the gospels and their pointing to a kingdom not of this world. By the same token, Schweitzer misses the import of Hinduism's pointing to a state which is beyond good and evil:

> To be exalted above the world means for the Brahmins: to be above all action, good as well as evil.[1]

> The Brahmins of the period of the Upanishads make no attempt to give ethical meaning to world or life denial and the mysticism of union with the Brahman.[2]

He interprets this as a despairing of life and as an exaltation of non-action over action. What it means however is that where good is set over against evil, life is fragmented. Whenever the ego takes action, whether it opts for good or for evil, it is unable to anneal the fissures which it creates. Thus non-action does not mean no action, but action in which the ego is not pitting itself dualistically against the world. It is action in which I act, yet not I, but *brahman* in me. Does not the Bible point to the same possibility of transcending dualism when it says: "To the pure all things are pure?" And does not the Beatitude suggest that this self-same transcendence of dualism is the prerequisite of the mystical vision: "Blessed are the pure in heart for they shall see God?"

To Schweitzer, dualism is the very heart of his ethical mysticism. His ethical mysticism is dualistic in the sense

[1]*Ibid.*, p. 43.
[2]*Ibid.*, p. 43.

that it presupposes two principles in the history of human life in this world. One is an ethical God who protects human ethical goals. The other is the impersonal power existing as nature. He sees the world as a battleground whereon ethical power contests with natural power. A religion can be considered as being monistic if its ultimate allegiance is to the totality of impersonal power. Thus, the monistic God is not separated from the natural forces and man can know God through the knowledge of the world. In this way, monism is in opposition to dualism:

> The theory of the Universe which these doctrinaire world-views represent is dualistic. They assume two principles in the history of events starting from the very origins of Being. One principle is conceived as an ethical personality who guarantees that what happens in the Universe has an ethical goal; the other is represented as the natural force dwelling within the Universe and operative in a course of events governed by natural laws. This dualistic world-view exists in very many variations. In the teaching of Zarathustra, in that of the Jewish prophets and in Christianity what happens in the Universe is interpreted as a battle in which the supernatural ethical power wins its way through in conflict with the natural non-ethical.[1]

> A religion is monistic if it considers God to be the sumtotal of all the forces at work in the universe, and, therefore, believes that in the knowledge of the universe we can attain to perfect knowledge of God. Thus, in its very nature, monism is pantheistic.[2]

For Schweitzer, the ethical God stands in direct contrast with the natural God, and there is an unbridgeable gulf between dualism and monism and between the ethical and the natural. That is why even when Hinduism as a monism seeks for an ethic, Schweitzer insists, it has never successfully attained to one:

> They strive for an ethic. They stretch out towards it in thought; but in the end they sink back exhausted. The

[1]*Ibid.*, pp. 11-12.
[2]Schweitzer, *Christianity and the Religions of the World*, pp. 39-40.

branch which they pulled down breaks in their hand and springs back, depriving them of the possibility to take hold of the fruit they had longed to pluck.[1]

He goes on to say:

That they ultimately take possession of it in words only, while in reality they allow it to slip, is here revealed with terrible clearness.[2]

To Schweitzer, Hinduism is both passive and pessimistic:

World and life negation on the other hand consists in his regarding existence as he experiences it in himself and as it is developed in the world as something meaningless and sorrowful, and he resolves accordingly (a) to bring life to a standstill in himself by mortifying his will-to-live, and (b) to renounce all activity which aims at improvement of the conditions of life in this world.[3]

By virtue of its passivity and pessimism, Hinduism is inferior to Christianity, Schweitzer claims in the conclusion of his book *Indian Thought and its Development,* and "the thought of mankind must advance to a position where it derives its world-view from ethics,"[4] for the ethical God is higher than the natural God. And thus it is quite natural for him to obey what the ethical God wills and to negate what the natural God urges. In order to do so, Schweitzer wills to fight both for the ethical and against the natural. To Schweitzer, it is contradictory that man is ethical and at the same time natural, but this situation cannot be allowed to remain:

I therefore recognize it as the destiny of my existence to be obedient to this higher revelation of the will-to-live in me. I choose for my work the removal of this division of the will-to-live against itself, so far as the influence of my existence

[1] *Ibid.,* pp. 78-79.
[2] *Ibid.,* p. 79.
[3] Schweitzer, *Indian Thought and Its Development,* pp. 1-2.
[4] *Ibid.,* p. 265.

reaches. Knowing now the one thing needful, I leave on
one side the enigma of the world and of my existence in it.[1]

Thus he would deal with the contradiction by fighting for
the victory of the ethical over the natural. It does not occur to him that the ultimate problem is not the intractabil-
ity of the natural to the ethical but rather the original separation between them. From the oriental point of view,
once life has been polarized as between the ethical and the
natural, the Fall has occurred and no victory of one over
the other can restore pristine harmony. For ethics to dominate nature is as sinful ultimately as for nature to dominate ethics.

Dualism also characterizes his conception of the relationship of self and other. To him, a life for others entails
the death of self. The life of the self must be suppressed
or repressed by the will-to-live for others. The life which is
suppressed is nothing but egoism, and it is natural egoism
from which Schweitzer wants to be free:

> Just as in the reverence for my own will-to-live I struggle
> for freedom from the destinies of life, so I struggle too for
> freedom from myself.[2]

Nature and ego together constitute the evil against which
he fights:

> The struggle against the evil that is in mankind we have to
> carry on not by judging others, but by judging ourselves.
> Struggle with oneself and veracity towards oneself are the
> means by which we work upon others.[3]

In the dualism of self and others, whoever shall lose his life
for others, the same shall find it again. This can be taken
to mean that whoever shall lose his selfish life, the same
shall find altruistic life:

Schweitzer, *Civilization and Ethics* (London: A & C. Black, Ltd., 1929),
250.
[2] *Ibid.*, p. 251.
[3] *Ibid.*, p. 253.

Ethics are reverence for the will-to-live within me and without me. From the former comes first the profound life-affirmation of resignation.[1]

Resignation is the vestibule through which we enter ethics. Only he who in deepened devotion to his own will-to-live experiences inward freedom from outward occurrences, is capable of devoting himself in profound and steady fashion to the life of others.[2]

A man is truly ethical only when he obeys the compulsion to help all life which he is able to assist, and shrinks from injuring anything that lives. He does not ask how far this or that life deserves one's interest as being valuable, nor, beyond that, whether and how far it can appreciate such interest. Life as such is sacred to him. He tears no leaf from a tree, plucks no flower, and takes care to crush no insect. If in summer he is working by lamplight, he prefers to keep the window shut and breathe a stuffy atmosphere rather than see one insect after another fall with singed wings upone his table.'[3]

To Schweitzer, it is a basic principle that man has to fight for good and against evil:

There we have given us that basic principle of the moral which is a necessity of thought: It is good to maintain and to promote life: it is bad to destroy life or to obstruct it.[4]

Although Schweitzer wants to help others according to his ethical principle, he ignores the necessity of the non-duality of self and other. No matter how much man may strive to help others, the goal can never be fulfilled by denying one's own ego. Here Schweitzer misses the point that man's existence for others is not merely ethical being which requires self-denial and socialization of the raw materials. Where altruism is seen as opposite to egoism, to live for others ethically necessitates the death of egoism. However, as far as human experience goes, to totally extirpate

[1]*Ibid.*, p. 251.
[2]*Ibid.*, p. 251.
[3]*Ibid.*, p. 247.
[4]*Ibid.*, p. 246.

the ego appears to be an impossibility. No matter how much man talks about good and endeavors to practice it accordingly, egoism or the natural can never be overcome in this way. As soon as altruism or ethics is pitted against egoism or the natural, it is no longer altruistic or ethical, and becomes another form of evil. It is because ethics is the fulfillment of an imperative that the ethical relationship of self and other lacks naturalness or grace.

The dichotomy of life-affirmation and life-denial cannot be a criticism for distinguishing one religion from another, since all religions are confronted with it and no religion has ever achieved a conceptual or theological resolution of it. All have erred at some periods in their histories by going too far in one direction or the opposite. All have engendered systems of self-understanding, expressing here the one emphasis and there the other. This is as true for Christianity as it is for Hinduism or Buddhism. It may be helpful to contrast Schweitzer's version of Hinduism with two others—one by a Hindu and one by an occidental—which present opposite evaluations of Hinduism even though at crucial points their readings of Hinduism are not so very far from Schweitzer's. Where Schweitzer is excessively taken with the ethical dimension of religion and insufficiently attentive to its spiritual aspects, Aldous Huxley and S. Radhakrishnan see Hinduism mainly as a spiritual discipline and find it praiseworthy for precisely the reason that Schweitzer finds it wanting.

For Huxley, religion seeks to transcend both the human and the natural, and to be united with the divine itself. The fulfillment of man is attainable neither through ethical activity alone nor through mastering of or accommodation to the naturalistic reality but in seeking the universal. To realize this universal in Huxley's eyes demands some kind of dissociation from the world of nature and of man. His ultimate is thus abstract, other-worldly and life denying in that it is set over against everything concrete and of this world and this life. In this way, Huxley is mainly concerned with the "timeless," the "unmanifest," and "impassible" even at the cost of getting rid of himself in order to fulfill man's true desire for the unitive knowledge of the Godhead. In his book, *The Perennial Philosophy,* Huxley applies this point of view to the major religions of mankind and in particular freqently attempts to document it from Indian religious thought:

> In the present section we shall confine out attention to but a single feature of this traditional psychology—the most important, the most emphatically insisted upon by all exponents of the Perennial Philosophy and, we may add, the least psychological. For the doctrine that is to be illustrated in this section belongs to autology rather than psychology—to the science, not of the personal ego, but of that eternal Self in the depth of particular, individualized selves, and identical with, or at least akin to, the divine Ground. Based upon the direct experience of those who have fulfilled the necessary conditions of such knowledge, this teaching is expressed most succinctly in the Sanskrit formula, *tat tvam asi* ("That art thou"); the Atman, or immanent eternal Self, is one with Brahman, the Absolute Principle of all existence; and the last end of every human being is to discover the fact for himself, to find out Who he really is.[1]

> The divine Ground of all existence is a spiritual Absolute, ineffable in terms of discursive thought, but (in certain circumstances) susceptible of being directly experienced and realized by the human being. This Absolute is the God-without-form of Hindu and Christian mystical phraseology. The last end of man, the ultimate reason for human existence, is unitive knowledge of the divine Ground—the knowledge that can come only to those who are prepared to "die to self" as so make room, as it were, for God.[2]

> Direct knowledge *of* the ground cannot be had except by union, and union can be achieved only by annihilation of the self-regarding ego, which is the barrier separating the "thou" from the "That."[3]

[1]Aldous Huxley, *The Perennial Philosophy* (New York: Meridian Books, The World Publishing Company, 1968), pp. 1-2.

[2]*Ibid.,* p. 21.

[3]*Ibid.,* p. 35.

Thus Huxley clearly demarcates the divinely absolute from the humanly relative. Although at times he speaks of a true Self or an "eternal Self in the depth of particular, individualized selves," Huxley mainly separates the eternal Self from particular selves. Duality of the divine and the human is ultimately duality of the Self and self. Thus Huxley believes that union of the divine and the human is not union of the eternal Self and the particular individual ego, but a union of the eternal Self, in the particular ego, and the divine Ground.

As a result, man's ultimate goal—that is, union of Self and Godhead—is inevitably in competition with man's immediate end which is his everyday life. The reason for man's existence does not lie in the immediate but in the ultimate. Man's last end for Huxley is "unitive knowledge of the divine Ground which is that of the universal." And for Huxley unitive knowledge comes to men who are prepared to die to self, that is, to individuality. He repeatedly asserts this negation of individual consciousness to be the essence of the Perennial Philosophy:

> For, as all exponents of the Perennial Philosophy have constantly insisted, man's obsessive consciousness of, and insistence on being, a separate self is the final and most formidable obstacle to the unitive knowledge of God. To be a self is, for them, the original sin, and to die to self, in feeling, will and intellect, is the final and all-inclusive virtue.[1]

Since the unitive knowledge of the divine Ground is man's ultimate goal, only those activities which conduce to it are for Huxley truly religious. In effect, Huxley eliminates most of what has passed for religious behavior in favor of "contemplation" which he calls "the higher prayer," and which is reached in the degree that one's individual self is transcended. For Huxley, then, mystical religion is higher than ethical religion and is in fact true religion:

[1] *Ibid.*, p. 36.

The divine eternal fullness of life can be gained only by those who have deliberately lost the partial, separative life of craving and self-interest, of egocentric thinking, feeling, wishing and acting. Mortification or deliberate dying to self is inculcated with an uncompromising firmness in the canonical writings of Christianity, Hinduism, Buddhism and most of the other major and minor religions of the world, and by every theocentric saint and spiritual reformer who has ever lived out and expounded the principles of the Perennial Philosophy.[1]

To him, those who attain the divine fullness of life are "regenerate." Huxley's man who is regenerate is opposed to ordinary "unregenerate man." The regenerate in its ultimate sense is divorced from all that is natural. In other words, Huxley's man cannot live with Wordsworth's man as well as Byron's man. In Huxley's criticism of them,[2] Huxley says that the natural cannot be identified with the universal. To Huxley, nature can only be used as a means to man's unitive knowledge of the universal.

Huxley's essentially dualistic mode of thought leads him into two heresies from the oriental point of view: the first is an abstract view of reality which sets it over against ordinary, everyday, individual existence. When reality is viewed in this objective fashion as another realm to be attained to, then the question comes up, by what means? And here Huxley commits a second and a practical error. He does not see the non-duality of means and ends and in his later years fell into the dangerous illusion that drugs might point the way to reality by releasing super-normal states of consciousness:

> . . . it had always seemed to me possible that, through hypnosis, for example, or autohypnosis, by means of systematic meditation, or else by taking the appropriate drug, I might so change my ordinary mode of consciousness as to be able to know, from the inside, what the visionary, the medium, even the mystic were talking about.[3]

[1] *Ibid.,* p. 96.
[2] See *ibid.,* p. 68.
[3] Aldous Huxley, *The Doors of Perception* (New York: Harper & Row, 1956), p. 14.

Two such methods exist. Neither of them is perfect; but both are sufficiently reliable, sufficiently easy and sufficiently safe to justify their employment by those who know what they are doing. In the first case the soul is transported to its far-off destination by the aid of a chemical—either mescalin or lysergic acid. In the second case, the vehicle is psychological in nature, and the passage to the mind's antipodes is accomplished by hypnosis. The two vehicles carry the consciousness to the same region; but the drug has the longer range and takes its passengers further into the *terra incognita*.[1]

Huxley took the first method in order to go beyond his ordinary mode of consciousness:

By a series of, for me, extremely fortunate circumstances I found myself, in the spring of 1953, squarely athwart that trail. One of the sleuths had come on business to California. In spite of seventy years of mescalin research, the psychological material at his disposal was still absurdly inadequate, and he was anxious to add to it. I was on the spot and willing, indeed eager, to be a guinea pig. Thus it came about that, one bright May morning, I swallowed four-tenths of a gram of mescalin dissolved in half a glass of water and sat down to wait for the results.[2]

The resulting "elevated" state of consciousness is clearly in opposition to ordinary consciousness and held up as something special and higher which excludes ordinary human concerns:

. . . I realized that I was deliberately avoiding the eyes of those who were with me in the room, deliberately refraining from being too much aware of them. One was my wife, the other a man I respected and greatly liked; but both belonged to the world from which, for the moment, mescaline had delivered me—the world of selves, of time, of moral judgements and utilitarian considerations, the world (and it was this aspect of human life which I wished, above all else, to forget) of self-assertion, of cocksureness, of overvalued words and idolatrously worshiped notions.[3]

[1]*Ibid.*, pp. 85-86.
[2]*Ibid.*, p. 12.
[3]*Ibid.*, p. 36.

This participation in the manifest glory of things left no room, so to speak, for the ordinary, the necessary concerns of human existence, above all for concerns involving persons. For persons are selves and, in one respect at least, I was now a Not-self, simultaneously perceiving and being the Not-self of the things around me.[1]

Huxley goes on to advocate the use of drugs as religious instrumentalities:

What is needed is a new drug which will relieve and console our suffering species without doing more harm in the long run than it does good in the short. Such a drug must be potent in minute doses and synthesizable. If it does not possess these qualities, its production, like that of wine, beer, spirits and tobacco will interfere with the raising of indispensable food and fibers. It must be less toxic than opium or cocaine, less likely to produce undesirable social consequences than alcohol or the barbiturates, less inimical to heart and lungs than the tars and nicotine of cigarettes. And, on the positive side, it should produce changes in consciousness more interesting, more intrinsically valuable than mere sedation or dreaminess, delusions of omnipotence or release from inhibition.[2]

Huxley does not go so far as to present the drug experience as the full equivalent of enlightenment or realization, but only as "potentially helpful":

I am not so foolish as to equate what happens under the influence of mescaline or of any other drug, prepared or in the future preparable, with the realization of the end and ultimate purpose of human life: Enlightenment, the Beatific Vision. All I am suggesting is that the mescaline experience is what Catholic theologians call "a gratuitous grace," not necessary to salvation but potentially helpful and to be accepted thankfully, if made available.[3]

Just what is the value is not altogether clear. Is it that the foretaste thus afforded will strongly motivate the taster

[1]*Ibid.*, p. 35.
[2]*Ibid.*, pp. 64-65.
[3]*Ibid.*, p. 73.

to go to the arduous task of seeking full enlightenment? Is there not an equal likelihood—man being as weak as he is—that the taster will become addicted to the tasting itself and will persist in the drug experience? Or would Huxley maintain that in itself the drug experience has value in that it transforms the being of the taster? But this has not been demonstrated. The drug experience is an experience; one goes into it and one comes out of it. The ego is not ontologically transcended; it is only temporarily laid aside. It is the ego which takes the drug causing the dream, and it is the ego which recalls the dream afterwards.

The deeper question is ignored by Huxley: Is reality the *object* of any state of consciousness whether normal or drug-induced? For the orient, reality is not an experience. It is being. It cannot be given to an experience or apprehended by a state of consciousness because these are less than the whole man. All talk of special or expanded modes of consciousness is but a distortion of oriental spirituality.

An extended attempt to rebut Schweitzer's charges against Hinduism is made by Radhakrishnan's in his *Eastern Religions and Western Thought*. He accuses Schweitzer of an oversimplification of Hindu religious thought as well as of the religious situation in general:

> All immense simplifications of the complicated patterns of reality are misleading. To divide peoples into those who will not accept the world at all and those who will accept nothing else is hardly fair. The many reservations which Schweitzer is obliged to make in applying his scheme of world affirmation and world negation as opposite categories of which one or the other must be denied show that it is not adequate to the facts.[1]

The fact is that Hinduism is not divorced from daily life, and Radhakrishnan cites with approval the favorable comparative estimate made of Hinduism by Sir George Birdwood:

[1]Sri Sarvepalli Radhakrishnan, *Eastern Religions and Western Thought* (London: Oxford University Press, 1967), p. 74.

'European Christianity, unfortunately through the accident
of the impatience of some of its early converts of the military discipline of Rome, was at its beginning placed in opposition to the general philosophical literary, artistic and
scientific culture of the Gentile world, and thenceforward
in more or less marked antagonism also to the the modern secular life of the west. Happily in India . . . the Brahmanical
religious life has never sundered itself from the daily working life of the laity, but is a component part of it and indis-
solubly bound up with it.[1]

'India may yet be destined to prepare the way for the reconciliation of Christianity with the world, and through the
practical identification of the spiritual with the temporal
life, to hasten the period of that third step forward in the
moral development of humanity, when there will be no divisions of race, or creed, or class, or nationality, between
men, by whatsoever name they may be called, for they will
all be one in the acknowledgement of their common
brotherhood, with the same reality, and sense of consequent responsibility, with which two thousand years ago,
they recognised the Fatherhood of God, and again, two
thousand years before that an exceptionally endowed tribe
of Semites, in the very heart of Anterior Asia, formulated
for all men, and for all time, the inspiring and elevating
doctrine of his unity.'[2]

For Radhakrishnan, Hinduism and Christianity are both
oriented towards a world beyond this one, and in that respect can both be called other-worldly:

Religion springs from the conviction that there is another
world beyond the visible and the temporal with which man
has dealings, and ethics require us to act in this world with
the compelling vision of another.[3]

Moreover, the ecstatic element is discernible not only in Indian religions but in Christianity as well:

[1]*Ibid.*, p. 74.
[2]*Ibid.*, pp. 74-75.
[3]*Ibid.*, pp. 82-83.

Any argument based on ecstatic phenomena will apply to all religions alike.[1]

For Radhakrishnan, Hinduism only partakes of the genuine character of all religion in giving its ultimate allegiance to a kingdom not of this world. World negation and world affirmation must be connected and to uphold either without the other is to present a truncated view of things:

> The heart of religion is that man truly belongs to another order, and the meaning of man's life is to be found not in this world but in more than historical reality. His highest aim is release from the historical succession denoted by birth and death. So long as he is lost in the historical process without a realization of the super-historical goal, he is only 'once born' and is liable to sorrow. God and not the world of history is the true environment of our souls. If we overlook this important fact, and make ethics or world affirmation independent of religion or world negation, our life and thought become condescending, though this condescension may take the form of social service or philanthrophy. But it is essentially a form of self-assertion and not real concern for the well-being of others.[2]

Hinduism is both this worldly and other worldly, both monistic and theistic, both ethical and supra-ethical; but Radhakrishnan does not clearly perceive that finally Hinduism proposes a way to overcome all these and all other dualisms. In other words, his reply to Schweitzer is not radical enough and his own grasp of Hinduism seems conditioned by occidental and Christian concepts. Admittedly, Radhakrishnan's interpretation of Hindu religious ideas conceives of the goal in terms of union with the infinite, while Schweitzer's conception of the spiritual union sees it as taking place in man's ethical will.

Schweitzer would have liked to be able to set up Hinduism as an abstract position opposite to his own: when he thinks of it as such, he criticizes it for being monistic, super-ethical and life-denying. At other times he sees it as

[1] *Ibid.*, p. 80.
[2] *Ibid.*, p. 83.

resisting such over-simplified pigeon-holing. Then he criticizes it as being illogical and inconsistent. "Hinduism," he says,

> possesses an astonishing capacity for overlooking or setting aside theoretical problems because from time immemorial it has lived in a state of compromise between monotheism and polytheism, between pantheism and theism, between world and life negation and world and life affirmation, and between supera-ethical and ethical ways of regarding things.[1]

That his problem with Hinduism is the result of his own limited conceptions, does not occur to him. Hinduism, in fact, is neither the clear-cut abstraction with which he sometimes seeks to equate it nor the tissue of inconsistencies which it seems to him to be at other times. It is rather something he will be precluded from grasping so long as he lacks the awareness of the inner drive of Hinduism towards that which is beyond dualism.

That the paths are many while the goal is one is an age-old theme in Hinduism. No one who understands it and who understands its basis can be astonished at the plurality of formulations apparent in Hinduism.

It is Schweitzer's rationalism which is offended by the Hindu sense of reality as that which eludes conceptualization. The conflict in truth is not between a religion which affirms life and one which denies life as Schweitzer supposes. It is rather a conflict between religion—which must ever go beyond reason and beyond ethics to find the source of grace—and Pelagianism which grasps life as a task to be accomplished by man. The Pelagian remains unreconciled to himself and to life until both have been transformed by his work. There is no acceptance of life as it is, and no reliance on grace. Oriental religion seeks the ultimate concord with life and the sageliness of the sage is just this harmonious rapport. But the outcome of Pelagianism can only be the ineradicable disparity between the world as actuality

---

[1]Schweitzer, *Indian Thought and Its Development*, pp. 223-224.

and the world as ideality envisaged. Schweitzer's words are not those of a man who has made ultimate peace with life:

> 'Only at quite rare moments have I felt really glad to be alive. I could not but feel with a sympathy full of regret all the pain that I saw around me, not only that of men, but of the whole creation.'[1]

> To these questions there is no answer. It remains a painful enigma for me that I must live with reverence for life in a world which is dominated by creative will which is also destructive will, and destructive will which is also creative.[2]

It will remain always an enigma whenever man tries to understand the whole life by any rule. To Schweitzer, reverence for life is more important than life itself, and he forgets the fact that life itself is the source of all beings and that it is even present in man. In other words, Schweitzer is so attached to the "rule of reverence for life" that he forgets the "creator" of all lives:

> The Maker of all things, self-luminous, all-pervading. He dwells always in the hearts of men. He is revealed by the negative teachings (of the Vedanta), discriminative wisdom, and the knowledge of Unity based upon reflection. They who know Him become immortal.[3]

For Hinduism, life is not something that issues from man's work and actions; it is rather that man and his works are real so far as they issue from that which dwells always in the heart. Hindu spirituality does not ask the seeker to choose a particular form of Hindu religious ideas but to aim at actualizing the life which is in him. This being its intent, it is simply beside the point for Schweitzer to find "some theoretical loophole in them which might give an opening to hostile criticism."[4]

[1] Quoted from Huston Smith, *The Religions of Man* (New York: Harper and Row, 1958), p. 99.

[2] Schweitzer, *Civilization and Ethics*, p. 250.

[3] *Śvetāśvatara Upanishad*, iv:17, as translated in Nikhilananda, *The Upanishads* (New York: Harper & Row, 1959), pp. 116-117.

[4] E. A. Burtt, "What can Western Philosophy Learn from India?" *Philosophy East and West*, Vol. 5 (October, 1955), p. 200.

Therefore, Hindu religiosity is not based on any ideality, which is incapable of actualization; it is a search for
the beyond that is within. Man's search for the ultimate in
India is a search for the ultimate which is within man. In
other words, the search for the ultimate is a search for the
non-duality of the ultimate and the immediate. Becoming
one with the ultimate is entirely different from "Be ye perfect even as your heavenly Father is perfect." Non-duality
is not the outcome of striving to imitate the divine perfection. It is realizing the perfection which is already in man.
Seen from this point of view, man's ultimate goal in India
is attained neither by moral effort nor by theological knowl-
ege nor by any other faculty:

> The eye does not go thither, nor speech, nor the mind. We
> do not know It; we do not understand how anyone can
> teach It. It is different from the known; It is above the un-
> known.[1]

Both the known and the unknown are outside man's inmost self, and thus are dualistic. Transcending both know-
edge and ignorance, the ultimate reality in Hinduism is
neither abstract nor concrete, but non-dual:

> It is the Ear of the ear, the Mind of the mind, the Speech
> of speech, the Life of life, and the Eye of the eye. Having
> detached the Self (from the sense-organs) and renounced
> the world, the wise attain to Immortality.[2]

The detachment and renunciation referred to are not to be
dualistically interpreted as a leave-taking from the world.
Hindu renunciation should not be identified with the denial
of life in this world. On the contrary, the *Bhagavad-Gita*
says:

> Not by leaving works undone does a man win freedom

---

[1]*Kena Upanishad,* i:3, as translated in Nikhilananda, *The Upanishads,* p.
231.
[2]*Kena Upanishad,* i:2, as translated in *ibid.,* p. 230.

> from (the bond of) works, nor by renunciation alone can
> he win perfection's prize.[1]

When the Hindu sense of reality refuses to equate it simply
with this world, that does not necessarily mean it opts for
detachment and against attachment. Aside from both detachment and attachment, Hindu religiosity aims at the
non-duality of detachment and attachment:

> For not for a moment can a man stand still and not work,
> for every man is powerless and made to work by the con-
> stituents born of Nature.[2]

> It is material Nature's constituents that do all works what-
> ever (works are done); (but) he whose self is by the ego
> fooled thinks, 'It is I who do.'[3]

Otherwise stated, what is sought is the living relatedness
of detachment and attachment, such living relatedness is
not merely relational in the sense that it occurs between
two objects. Rather it is the original non-duality of *A* and
Not-A. In other words, non-duality is not a oneness which
opposes itself to a possible twoness. Instead, it is One without any second. And that One is known as Self:

> The Self, indeed, is below. It is above. It is behind. It is be-
> fore. It is to the south. It is to the north. The Self, indeed,
> is all this.[4]

The Self is the center of man. It is his original undivided
life. So if Hinduism turns away from this world, it should
not be taken to mean that there is something more
alongside the material world. That would only be setting
up an opposite to the material world and reality is not one
of two opposites. In other words, if reality is not A,
neither is it identifiable as Not-A. Neither would affirmation nor world-denial yield reality, but only that which is

---

[1]*Bhagavad-Gītā,* iii:4, as translated in R. C. Zaehner (Oxford: The
Clarendon Press, 1969), p. 162.

[2]*Bhagavad-Gītā,* iii:5, as translated in *ibid.,* p. 163.

[3]*Bhagavad-Gītā,* iii:27, as translated in *ibid.,* p. 171.

[4]*Chandogya Upanishad,* vii:25, 2, as translated in Nikhilananda, *The Upanishads,* vol. 4, p. 354.

neither affirmation nor denial. And that for Hinduism is to
grasp life and oneself whole and entire without any split
into A and Not-A. In this way, Hinduism points to the
spiritual without eliminating the material:

> Exalted are the senses, or so they say; higher than the
> senses is the mind; yet higher than the mind the soul: what
> is beyond the soul is he.[1]

In short, the essence of Hindu religiosity lies in pointing to
wholeness.

The artificial divisions between the ethical and the non-
ethical, between higher self and lower self, between this
world and other world, between life-affirmation and life-ne-
gation are witnesses to a basic inner dichotomy of the cultural and the natural, of duty and desire, of reason and passion, and the active and the passive within human beings.
As far as human experience goes, man can never remain in
permanent onesidedness. The fact of human history is that
man can never lend himself fully to any one pole of any
pair of opposites, and hence history shows a perpetual os-
cillation between the poles. The more one generation is
moralistic, the more the next is uncomfortable with it, and
impelled to establish its own culture on naturalistic
grounds. What history reveals is that it is utterly impossible for men to identify themselves fully with either pole of
any opposition, and whenever they pretend to do so,
sooner or later the pendulum swings to the opposite.

Hindu religiosity is surely not to be merely ethical. Nor
does it equate life with the natural. To Schweitzer, ethical
life is seen as fighting life. He imposes his will upon himself, on others, and on nature. But the oriental sees life not
in fighting life but in the graceful rapport with life. It is the
central meaning of grace that life is not something fully
manageable or malleable and that a yielding is called for.
This is also a corollary non-duality of the human and the
divine. As soon as man is separated from the divine, his
life is not graceful. He is set over against life and involved

---

[1]*Bhagavad-Gita,* iii:42, as translated in Zaehner, *Bhagavad-Gita,* p. 177.

in fighting it. Seen from the Hindu point of view, man's task is not merely to revere life but also to live wholly. For Schweitzer, ethical life alone is sacred but to the Hindu life itself—regardless of its quality—is sacred.

Hindu spirituality is thus not any collection of ideas to be compared with another collection called Christianity. It is a way to the One which is all in all. Thus, in the final analysis, it is not a possession of Hindus. And so Hinduism has no need to move along the way towards the truth as envisaged by Schweitzer:

> The pathway from imperfect to perfect recognised truth leads through the valley of reality. European thought has already descended into this valley. Indian thought is still on the hill on this side of it. If it wishes to climb to the hill beyond, it must first go down into the valley.[1]

Perfection in the Hindu sense is not to be sought at the end of history nor in any historical event or process. It is to be realized in oneself. There is no need to say "Be ye perfect even as your Heavenly Father is perfect," for the reason that man's perfection in its truest sense of the word is not differentiated from God's perfection. Perfection in every way is divine:

> Whatever being shows wider power, prosperity, or strength, be sure that this derives from (but) a fragment of my glory.[2]

Hindu religiosity lies in man's search for the ultimate that is within. The central thrust of Hindu religious thought will never be grasped deeply, so long as one approaches it as Schweitzer did as a body of "dead-cold data and static external observables in human behavior or as 'enemy territory' which must be reconnoitered in order to be conquered with the least possible effort."[3]

---

[1]Schweitzer, *Indian Thought and Its Development,* pp. 256-257.

[2]*Bhagavad-Gita,* x:41, as translated in Zaehner, *Bhagavad-Gita,* p. 302.

[3]Ismáil Ragi A. al Faruqi, *Christian Ethics* (Montreal: McGill University Press, 1967), pp. 8-9.

In Schweitzer, the inwardness of Hinduism has been greatly distorted and largely misconceived as a consequence of his dualistic rendering. Whenever he accepts anything as true, he believes that its opposite must be false and that consistency demands a detaching of oneself from this opposite. To such a dualistic consciousness, it is hardly plausible that Hindu spirituality is so truly universal and all-embracing that it cannot be identified with any form of objective knowledge or doctrine. In this sense, Schweitzer's understanding of Hindu religious thought is mainly external.

CHAPTER IV

INTERPRETING BUDDHISM

Buddhism, in contrast with Hinduism, had its origin in a particular man, but it went on to become a universal religion. It has peacefully penetrated the entire Far East without recourse to any form of violence. At the same time, it has exhibited the greatest flexibility in respect of form. Its universal characteristic is not opposed to its particular forms, and it has allowed itself to be diversified in accordance with the different cultures which it has permeated.

Gautama, unlike Jesus, was the son of a king, and thus endowed with virtually everything men ordinarily seek. Objectively he lacked nothing. And yet, after enjoying this life as given a period of nearly three decades, it finally became a burning problem to him, and he was driven to quest after its secret. To understand his quest and the meaning of Buddhism, we need to face his question: what do we lack when we possess everything? The answer is reality—which is not a possession. The quest of Buddhism is to grasp the ungraspable and is to enter into a reality which is not to be owned but the lack of which leaves all possessions ultimately unsatisfying. It is neither by owning nor by disowning, neither by affirming possessions nor by denying them that one enters into the truth, but by breaking through the dichotomy. This awareness is the substance of living Buddhism, and the essence of *bodhi;* enlightenment is the awakening to non-duality.

Without the basic understanding of the nonduality of

owning and disowning or of affirming possessions and denying them, interpretations of Buddhism will see it as a form
of oriental stoicism. Thus Arthur Schopenhauer expressed
the friendliest of sentiments towards Buddhist religious
thought precisely because he took it as fundamentally
kindred to his own philosophy. For this reason, he deemed
Buddhism as superior to other religions:

> If I wished to take the results of my philosophy as the stan-
> dard of truth, I should have to concede to Buddhism pre-
> eminence over the others. In any case, it must be a plea-
> sure to me to see my doctrine in such close agreement with
> a religion that the majority of men on earth hold as their
> own, for this numbers far more followers than any other.[1]

Taking the First Noble Truth of Buddhism as the asser-
tion of a metaphysical truth, he sees Buddhism as confirma-
tory of his own pessimistic rendering of life. That life is suffering is for Buddhism, however, neither a necessary nor
an ultimate statement, but only the *terminus a quo* of the
religious quest. The First Noble Truth for Buddhism characterizes the quality of unenlightened life, that is, life
alienated from its ground. The aim of Buddhism is to cope
with this quality of life at this level by overcoming the alienation from the ground of being. One who is enlightened,
that is, one who lives from the ground of being rather than
from his own ego, is not plagued by the First Noble Truth.

For Schopenhauer, however, suffering is a characteristic ingrained in life and the problem of suffering can be resolved only by denying life:

> All satisfaction, or what is commonly called happiness, is
> really and essentially always *negative* only, and never posi-
> tive. It is not a gratification which comes to us originally
> and of itself, but it must always be the satisfaction of a
> wish. For desire, that is to say, want, is the precedent con-
> dition of every pleasure; but with the satisfaction, the de-
> sire and therefore the pleasure cease; and so the satisfac-
> tion or gratification can never be more than deliverance

---

[1]Arthur Schopenhauer, *The World as Will and Representation* (The Falcon's Wing Press, 1958), Vol. II, p. 169.

from a pain, from a want. Such is not only every actual
and evident suffering, but every desire whose importunity
disturbs our peace, and indeed even the deadening bore-
dom that makes existence a burden to us.[1]

Anyone who has awakened from the first dreams of youth;
who has considered his own and others' experience; who
has looked at life in the history of the past and of his own
time, and finally in the works of the great poets, will certainly acknowledge the result, if his judgment is not
paralysed by some indelibly imprinted prejudice, that this
world of humanity is the kingdom of chance and error.
These rule in it without mercy in great things as in small;
and along with them folly and wickedness also wield the
scourge. . . . But as regards the life of the individual, every
life-history is a history of suffering, for, as a rule, every life
is a continual series of mishaps great and small, concealed
as much as possible by everyone, because he knows that
others are almost always bound to feel satisfaction at the
spectacle of annoyances from which they are for the moment exempt; rarely will they feel sympathy or compassion. . . . The essential purport of the world-famous
monologue in *Hamlet* is, in condensed form, that our state
is so wretched that complete non-existence would be de-
cidedly preferable to it. Now if suicide actually offered us
this, so that the alternative "to be or not to be" lay before
us in the full sense of the words, it could be chosen uncon-
ditionally as a highly desirable termination ("a consummation devoutly to be wished").[2]

By the same token, Schopenhauer sees Buddhism as essentially the denial of the will to live. According to
Schopenhauer, the Buddhist ideal is to attain a state in
which there is no conditioning by birth, old-age, disease
and death. He identified such a state as the Buddhist
nirvana. To attain this state of *nirvana,* it seemed to
Schopenhauer that asceticism and mortification of will are
necessary. Man's voluntary and intentional denial of will
to live are directed towards alleviating the suffering of life.
Denial of the will to live culminates in dying:

[1]*Ibid.,* Vol. I, p. 319.
[2]*Ibid.,* p. 324.

Dying is the moment of that liberation from the onesidedness of an individuality which does not constitute the inner-
most kernel of our true being, but is rather to be thought
of as a kind of aberration thereof. The true original freedom again enters at this moment which in the sense stated
can be regarded as a *restitutio in integrum*. The peace and
composure on the countenance of most dead people seem
to have their origin in this. As a rule, the death of every
good person is peaceful and gentle; but to die willingly, to
die gladly, to die cheerfully, is the prerogative of the
resigned, or him who gives up and denies the will-to-live.
For he alone wishes to die *actually* and not merely *appar-
ently,* and consequently needs and desires no continuance
of his person. He willingly gives up the existence that we
know; what comes to him instead of it is in our eyes *nothing,* because our existence in reference to that one is *nothing.* The Buddhist faith calls that existence *Nirvana,* that is
to say, extinction.[1]

To him, not only Buddhism but also Christianity is pessimistic:

I cannot, as is generally done, put the *fundamental difference* of all religions in the question whether they are
monotheistic, polytheistic, pantheistic, or atheistic, but
only in the question whether they are optimistic or pessimistic, in other words, whether they present the existence of
this world as justified by itself, and consequently praise
and commend it, or consider it as something which can be
conceived only as the consequence of our guilt, and thus
ought not to be, in that they recognize that pain and death
cannot lie in the eternal, original, and immutable order of
things, that which in every respect ought to be. The power
by virtue of which Christianity was able to overcome first
Judaism, and then the paganism of Greece and Rome, is to
be found solely in its pessimism, in the confession that our
condition is both exceedingly sorrowful and sinful, whereas
Judaism and paganism were optimistic.[2]

The Hegelians, who regard the philosophy of history as
even the main purpose of all philosophy, should be
referred to Plato, who untiringly repeats that the object of

[1]*Ibid.,* Vol. II, p. 508.
[2]*Ibid.,* p. 170.

philosophy is the unchangeable and ever permanent, not that which now is thus and then otherwise. All who set up such constructions of the course of the world, or, as they call it, of history, have not grasped the principle truth of all philosophy, that that which is is at all times the same, that all becoming and arising are only apparent, that the Ideas alone are permanent, that time is ideal. This is what Plato means, this is what Kant means. Accordingly, we should try to understand what *exists*, what actually *is*, today and always, in other words, to know the *Ideas* (in Plato's sense). On the other hand, fools imagine that something is supposed to come into existence. They therefore concede to history a principle place in their philosophy and construct this on an assumed plan of the world, according to which everything is managed for the best. This is then supposed to appear *finaliter*, and will be a great and glorious thing. Accordingly, they take the world to be perfectly real, and set its purpose in miserable earthly happiness. Even when it is greatly cherished by man and favoured by fate, such happiness is yet a hollow, deceptive, frail, and wretched thing, out of which neither constitutions, legal systems, steam-engines, nor telegraphs can ever make anything that is essentially better. Accordingly, the aforesaid philosophers and glorifiers of history are simple realists, and also optimists and eudaemonists, and consequently shallow fellows and Philistines incarnate. In addition, they are really bad Christians, for the true spirit and kernel of Christianity, as of Brahmanism and Buddhism also, is the knowledge of the vanity of all earthly happiness, complete contempt for it, and the turning away to an existence of quite a different, indeed an opposite, kind. This, I say, is the spirit and purpose of Christianity, the true "humour of the matter"; but it is not, as they imagine, monotheism. Therefore, atheistic Buddhism is much more closely akin to Christianity than are optimistic Judaism and its variety, Islam.[1]

Pure Christianity has essentially the same view of life as Buddhism, but historic Christianity has been compromised by Judaic optimism, as well as by Roman and European worldliness. Hence,

[1]*Ibid.*, pp. 443-444.

In India our religions will never at any time take root; the ancient wisdom of the human race will not be supplanted by the events in Galilee. On the contrary, Indian wisdom flows back to Europe, and will produce a fundamental change in our knowledge and thought.[1]

Salvation then comes from man's denial of the will to live, and affirmation of the will to live is original sin:

This original sin itself is in fact the affirmation of the will-to-live; on the other hand, the denial of this will, in consequence of the dawning of better knowledge, is salvation.[2]

Thus, he insisted that naive optimism is not religious:

At bottom, optimism is the unwarranted self-praise of the real author of the world, namely of the will-to-live which complacently mirrors itself in its work. Accordingly optimism is not only a false but also a pernicious doctrine, for it presents life as a desirable state and man's happiness as its aim and object.[3]

Thus, for Schopenhauer, authentic religion is inevitably pessimistic. Optimism is always something separated from a religious search for reality. The denial of the will to live is the essence of the spiritual, and redemption lies in "not to be."

Nevertheless, the issue of pessimism or optimism is confused by Schopenhauer. Pessimism may be taken to mean that the world is irredeemably bad, and optimism may be taken to mean that it is good as it is. But no religion teaches either. Both Judaeo-Christianity and Buddhism would be anti-pessimistic as well as anti-optimistic in this sense. Or, if one merely means to assert that unredeemed, the world, is evil but redemption is possible and afterwards the evil is overcome, then Buddhism, Christianity, Judaism and Islam are optimistic and pessimistic.

Does redemption take man out of the world or is the world itself to be redeemed? The problem of this-worldly sal-

[1]*Ibid.*, Vol. I, p. 357.
[2]*Ibid.*, Vol. II, p. 608.
[3]*Ibid.*, p. 584.

vation and other-worldly salvation is also begged by
Schopenhauer. For example, the Hinayana idea of *nirvana*
is rather other-worldly, escapistic, and pessimistic. The
Mahayana idea of *nirvana,* on the other hand, is that of a
this-worldly, optimistic transfiguration of *samsara.* It is not
clear that Schopenhauer was aware of the distinction or of
the issues involved.

Schopenhauer's stance is stoical rather than religious—he opts for one pole—to fight the will to live. However, religion in the oriental sense of the word, does not
seek absoluteness at one pole of a dichotomy. Buddhism
recommends neither fighting nor surrendering. It requests
neither that thy will be done nor does it demand that mine
shall be done. Buddhism in its living reality is neither the
indulgence of the will nor mortification of it. Rather it is
the middle way.

This has a twofold meaning. Its literal meaning is an
avoidance of extremes—in this sense of pessimism and
optimism, but its deepest meaning is to be found in the non-
duality of opposites. Reality is discernible neither in affirmation, nor in denial, nor through compromise between
them but only in the integral life which is not thus sundered. Of this primal wholeness, Buddhism would say
"What has been from the beginning joined together, let no
man rend asunder." This, Schopenhauer was very far from
understanding.

Subsequent interpretations of Buddhism have more
often than not been along the lines of Schopenhauer's pessimistic interpretation. F. Nietzsche,[1] Max Scheler,[2] W. L.
King and Henri de Lubac have all seen Buddhist religious
ideas from the perspective of pessimism. For example,
King is a fairly typical representative of recent Protestant

[1]See Friedrich Nietzsche, *Beyond Good and Evil,* ed. by Oscar Levy (London: T. N. Foulis, 1914), pp. 81-83.

Also see *Birth of Tragedy,* Vol. III (London: George Allen & Unwin,
Ltd., 1924), p. 158.

[2]See Max Scheler, *The Nature of Sympathy* (London: Routledge & Kegan
Paul, 1970), passim.

interpretation in approach of Buddhism, while de Lubac may be regarded as a fairly typical representative of Catholic interpretation of Buddhism. Both King and de Lubac agree with Schopenhauer's pessimistic interpretation of Buddhism as Schweitzer does, although they would reject his pessimistic rendition of Christianity.

In contrast to Schopenhauer, both of them think that religion in its true nature should be optimistic and that Christianity is such. Buddhism, unlike Christianity, is said to be based on a pessimistic outlook on life in this world, and thus it is considered to be inferior to Christianity.

In his *Buddhism and Christianity,* King offers a comparative study of Buddhism in relation to Christianity. King, first of all, rejects the approach of "radical displacement" as that has been described by Professor Hocking. Neither Buddhism nor Christianity can be the only religion acceptable to mankind. That the Buddhist *dharma* alone can save the world is as dogmatic and as unlikely as the notion that Christian faith alone can redeem mankind. He rejects both expressions of radical displacement:

> Since the central thesis of this work is that it is both possible and desirable to attempt to throw bridges of understanding across the centuries-old chasm between Buddhism and Christianity—and not just for the instrumental purpose of gaining converts from the other side—I cannot fully accept either of the above statements (Buddhism or Christian) as the final word on the matter.[1]

King described himself as a liberal Protestant with an essentially dialogical understanding of the two religions:

> Of course, something of the same difficulty also relates to the use of the word "Christian" as a descriptive adjective in view of a like variety within Christendom. And the author must plead guilty to using the term with regard to what *he* understands the central Christian tradition to be—though his background and perspective is that of liber-

[1]Winston Lee King, *Buddhism and Christianity* (Philadelphia: The Westminster Press, mcmlxii), p. 18.

al Protestant, which inevitably colors the interpretation here given to Christianity.[1]

Thus his aim is neither syncretistic nor exclusivistic, but to foster inter-communication:

The attempt here is hopefully to avoid these extremes in the interest of some sort of genuine dialogue.[2]

Although limiting his study to Theravada Buddhism, he shows awareness of the perils of comparative studies which limit themselves to externals and which ignore the inwardness of one or both of the religious being considered:

To make such exploration of the interfaith terrain meaningful, there must be a genuine attempt to understand the strange faith "in depth," avoiding the merely superficial similarities and differences, trying to relate religious deep to religious deep in accordance with actual function and essence in each respective faith.[3]

King seems to have some understanding of the difficulties of conveying the Buddhist sense of life:

Buddhism approaches *its* ultimates in terms of negatives. The profoundest truths, it affirms, cannot be arrived at by reasoning but by intuitive perceptions. The highest wisdom cannot be communicated by word; it is more often realized in silence. Ultimate realities—such as Nirvana—are absolutely indescribable. Qualifying phrases, descriptions, conceptualization may even distort or hide its true nature, and their mouthing becomes a substitute for the fullness of the reality itself. Truth in the ultimate sense is *realized*, not *known*.[4]

The essence of Buddhism is inexpressible, and thus it cannot be known. It must be realized. Accordingly, for King, Buddhism can only be silent about its ultimacy.

Is Buddhist silence a symptom of ultimate ignorance or

[1]*Ibid.*, p. 11.
[2]*Ibid.*, p. 9.
[3]*Ibid.*, p. 19.
[4]*Ibid.*, p. 27.

of a knowledge intent on keeping its secret? Does silence stand in opposition to utterance or rhetoric? However one answers these questions he will be unjust to Buddhism, for the questions themselves come from dualistic presupposition. King misses the depth of Buddhist silence. Silence, as a Buddhist conceives of it, is not a state which is opposed to other states. It is to Buddhists neither ignorance nor a sign of realization. But it is reality itself—which is not fragmented. This silence is no closer to ignorance than it is to knowledge. Nor is it closer to agnosticism than it is to atheism or theism. It is not simply keeping quiet but the non-duality of the knower and the known or the seeker and the sought. In this sense, silence is man's existential openness to reality which is not a posession. And thus it is not simply a means by which ultimacy can be attained. King misunderstands it, when he says: "But the truly Real cannot be described save by silence."[1] The Buddha's smile is neither the opposite of anger nor a facial movement. But it is a smile which is one with Buddha's whole being, and it is the presence of his whole being. Seen from this point of view, the smile is not an artificial make-up but ringing truth. Without understanding the non-duality of silence and utterance, of affirming and denying, of smiling and anger, King sees Buddhism as mere silence, denial of utterance, and passivity. Such an interpretation of Buddhism culminates in the denial of ultimate reality, and thus King sees Buddhism as atheism:

> Southern Buddhism insists that the Buddha is essentially Ideal Man and flatly denies the existence of a Supreme God in any form whatsoever.[2]

> The central core of Buddhism both in theory and practice tends to remain nontheistic in the strict sense. Nor should we seek to evade or deny the strength of the Buddhist nontheistic conviction despite practical flaws in its purity. To repeat in part what was said in the previous chapter, we may observe that Buddhism does indeed deny that there is

[1]*Ibid.*, p. 49.
[2]*Ibid.*, p. 34.

a Supreme and Almighty God in all the forms with which that doctrine has been clothed: First Cause, Unmoved Mover, Creator, Almighty Father, Supreme Being, Spiritual Presence, All Knower, etc., etc.[1]

However, one might properly use the term "divine atheism" with regard to Buddhism, not so much in the sense of approving the high purity of its atheism, but rather in the sense of a "spiritual" or "religious" atheism. For this is precisely what even the most purely atheistic Buddhism is—a deeply religious atheism.[2]

Characterizing Buddhism as atheism, King tries to find a God-substitute in Buddhism:

Much might be said along this line, but the above may suffice to suggest that there is more in Buddhist "atheism" than the mere word itself suggests. And this calls for further examination. We shall therefore turn our attention to four factors that form what I shall call a *reality-complex* or *reality-structure,* namely, Dharma, Karma, Nirvana, and the Buddha. These four elements embrace the highest order of realities that we can find in Buddhist theory and practice. And our interest here will be to note if, and in what way, they work together to provide a God-substitute or fulfill a God-function in Buddhism.[3]

As a result of his analysis of these concepts, he concedes that the four central items do not function in the same way as the God conceived of by Christianity. To King, Nirvana can be God in human experience, but it cannot be the God of history. And therefore, *nirvana* can never be a divine person who created the world and man:

Nirvana in the Buddhist God-or-religious-experience, is not of history, theological description, or of morality. These latter functions of Deity, which the Christian mystic took for granted as the ordinary context of his mystical experience, the Buddhist refers to the areas of Dharma, Karma, and Buddha, but does *not* include in the Nirvana context.[4]

[1]*Ibid.,* p. 35.
[2]*Ibid.,* p. 37.
[3]*Ibid.,* p. 38.
[4]*Ibid.,* pp. 57-58.

The lack of a God substance, King claims, leaves Buddhism without the unifying power of one-god-over-all-things:

> We must therefore ask, of what sort is the essential unity of the Dharma-Karma-Nirvana-Buddha complex? And we must reply—a point that the Christian must always keep in mind when thinking of Buddhism—that the result is a kind of loose-jointed deity complex rather than any entity that can be called God in the Christian sense. The complex does *not* have the tight integrality that Christianity has sought to achieve in its concept of God and in its distinctive religious experience. This Buddhist "God-complex" in its four parts works differently, and perhaps even antagonistically within itself, for different purposes at different levels and under different conditions.[1]

The question may well be put: Is King arguing for the superiority of the Christian concept of God over the Buddhist concept? Or is he claiming that the Christian is closer to reality than the Buddhist? In either case, does he have an independent cirticism other than his own Christian concept of God?

King has not perceived Buddhism as beyond the duality of denying and affirming. For example, Buddhism affirms neither deity nor non-deity. The typical occidental cannot envisage a real alternative to theism and atheism *Tertium non datur*. Agnosticism merely side-steps the issue, and in any case, Buddhism is no more to be equated with agnosticism—which is only a "position"—than with theism or atheism. King equates Buddhism with atheism. Thereby, he forgets that all verbal usage in Buddhism is pedagogical and not meant to convey ultimate truth.

Buddhism does not take a philosophical or theological position. King forgets what he said about silence in Buddhism as he overlooks the difference between Buddhist philosophy and Buddhism as religious life. And thus despite himself he takes a stand against Buddhism, and distorts his original dialogic intention. It seems often extreme-

[1] *Ibid.*, p. 58.

ly difficult for occidental man not to imagine that "those who are not for me are against me," and that one can say in reference to theism as well as to atheism "a plague on both your houses." From King's dualistic standpoint, he finds hidden conflicts in the reality-structure of Buddhism:

> For they are not integrally one order but are even antithetically opposed to each other at times. There is the tension between dharma and karma, for example. Dharma is the impersonal, nonmoral causality found in the order of nature. But karma is an absolutely just and impartial *moral* order. The two obviously clash at many points, since the natural order brings calamity, disease, death, pain, and the like upon seemingly undeserving individuals. Yet Buddhists faith makes them one by insisting that even the natural order serves ethical ends, i.e., that whatever comes to a man, either pleasant *or* unpleasant, is *morally* deserved because of his past lives. Yet in order to avoid the theistic problem of evil (God both good and almighty) the Buddhist turns again and insists that the moral order that punishes evil and rewards good is essentially only impersonal, scientifically perceived causality such as is found also in the natural order.[1]

> But there is further an even more serious tension between dharma-karma and Nirvana. The first has to do with the order of mundane life whose main goal is the achievement of more pleasant rebirths of individual beings in space-time worlds, and whose only means of advancement is through ethical good deeds. Here is the way of the devout Buddhist layman. But the Way of Nirvana is one of meditation, detachment from individual persons and worldly goals and values whether good or evil. The goodness that it seeks is above, or different from, ordinary ethical goodness and its goal is far beyond history and the improvement of society. This is the way of the monk. Thus the Buddhist cosmos is split between the nonnatural, nontemporal, nonethical, nonhistorical order of Nirvana (and the way to it) and the natural, temporal, ethical, and historical order of dharma-karma (and the way to better rebirths). One pays his currency of ethical-historical action, or of meditative detachment and takes his choice.[2]

[1]*Ibid.*, p. 59.
[2]*Ibid.*, pp. 59-60.

But has Christian thought escaped these conceptual tensions? What about the opposition of contemplative and the active life? What of the dualism of the natural and the human, of impersonal and personal, of the earthly and the heavenly, layman and monk, or good and evil? Can Christianity be exclusively identified with either pole of any of the dichotomous renditions of its self-understanding? Likewise Buddhism is not identifiable with a metaphysical or theological position. It is not closer to monism than it is to pluralism, and is not to be characterized either as atheism or as theism. King is ignoring the history and scriptures of Christianity when he asserts simply that:

> The Christian doctrine of creativity puts God squarely in the middle of the world process. This joins natural and historical orders of the world. The world as we know it, and live in it, is thereby considered essentially good and worthy of redemption; and the Christian faith in God, as seen in Christ, is that there is an active work of redemption going on in the midst of this world and its life.[1]

King, on the other hand, concedes that enlightened Buddhists do achieve existentially the living non-duality of the opposites which thought and speech cannot bring together:

> This multiplicity of level of operation and diversity of form in the complex which fulfills the God-function for Buddhism is perhaps lessened in two respects. First, the saints and the Buddhas represent in their lives a joining of this diversity into one kind of unity. For they do indeed live in the space-time world (dharma-karma realm), and have in the past followed *its* ways of virtue, progressing even as others from birth to birth. Yet, building on this basis of dharma-karma, causal-moral order, they have also achieved nirvanic stature, or have escaped the former order of life for the latter; and for one last lifetime they live as Nirvana-experiences in the world of dharma-karma. Thus they are in the world of dharma-karma and rebirth, but not of it.[2]

[1]*Ibid.,* p. 62.
[2]*Ibid.,* p. 60.

> And secondly, there is a current tendency in Buddhism to join the two ways of life (dharmic and nirvanic) in one, in the form of the life of worldly (layman's) activity *and* simultaneous periodic meditation periods by that same lay-man.[1]

He is not led to ponder the implications of this fact. If he really does believe that Buddhist saints have achieved "nirvanic stature" while being in the world, does this imply that Buddhism is a way to reality or not? And if it is, what does it matter about its concepts seeing that the whole effort of Buddhism is to go beyond concepts to realization?

He calls attention to what is for him another serious fissure in Buddhism.

> There is the world of ordinary moral virtue and social action, but it is separated from the world of ultimate spiritual worth (Nirvana) as by a chasm; the lesser and the higher goods have no integral relation to each other. Thus in the end the lack of an integral God-concept atomizes the Buddhist world and makes significant life-unity—save on a purely individualistic level—most difficult. Those positively creative and helpful aspects of the world process, which the Christian calls God, can be acknowledged only indirectly under cover of one's "own" karmic merit, if at all.[2]

But he concedes that Christianity has its own difficulties in reconciling its ultimates:

> Which set of difficulties is the preferable one—the Christian God concept, whose internal tensions of power versus goodness, and of impersonal natural order created by personal being, tend to explode it; or the Buddhist reality-complex, which achieves no integral unity of inner and outer lives and can scarcely frame a unifying philosophy of historical action—is perhaps a question that requires considerable study and further experience. And in the end its answer for the individual may depend upon his personal choice of religious values.[3]

[1] *Ibid.,* p. 60.
[2] *Ibid.,* p. 63.
[3] *Ibid.,* p. 63.

If no concepts, neither Christian nor Buddhist, are finally adequate to the fullness of reality, and if some Buddhists do experientially and existentially realize the truth of non-duality and do achieve "nirvanic stature," then what is the significance of King's claim that:

> . . . despite these unitive tendencies, no full integral synthesis of a divine world order is ever wholly or explicitly achieved?[1]

Whatever else the absolute may be, it cannot be something which is utterly divorced from one's own existence. It cannot merely be in history or in the world, because it would then not be existentially rooted in self. A god of history is a divinity who forgets man's personal existence, and does not relate directly to man's own self. No matter how much one talks about God-substance in the mode adapted by King, that of itself does not set free! Only a god who is inseparable from one's own living and concrete existence can be liberating. A general concept of God has unity and meaning, insofar as it can be shared with others, but an idea is something possessed. A God who is possessed cannot liberate his possessor. The God who alone sets man free is not one to be conceptualized, but realized with man's whole being. Such a God may be lived, (and then one attains "nirvanic stature"), but is not to be objectified. God in Buddhism is no closer to nature than history. God is man's true being, and vice versa. Thus ultimate reality is not a substance over against man, ut the non-duality of man and God. This non-duality ?epens life while dualism limits life.

In contrast to King's interpretation, Edward Conze af- ms that Buddhism has an ontological ground. To Conze, iddhism is fundamentally based on Godhead:

> When we compare the attributes of the Godhead as they are understood by the more mystical tradition of Christian

[1]*Ibid.*, pp. 60-61.

thought, with those of Nirvana, we find almost no difference at all.[1]

We are told that Nirvana is permanent, stable, imperishable, immovable, ageless, deathless, unborn, unbecome, that it is power, bliss and happiness, the secure refuge, the shelter, and the place of unassailable safety; that it is the real Truth and the supreme Reality; that it is the Good, the supreme goal and the one and only consummation of our life, the eternal, hidden and incomprehensible Peace.[2]

Similarly, the Buddha who is, as it were, the personal embodiment of Nirvana, becomes the object of all those emotions which we are wont to call religious.[3]

Conze thus affirms that Buddhism, like Christianity, has a definite concept of God-substance. Although Conze differs from King in this regard, both of them agree with the fact that Buddhism is essentially pessimistic:

Our human nature, according to the Buddhist contention, is so constituted that we are content with nothing but complete permanence, complete ease, complete security. And none of that can we ever find in this shifting world.[4]

On the basis of this pessimistic version of Buddhism, King misconceives the significance of Buddhist morality:

. . . such attitudes are *primarily* considered by Buddhism to be good *in terms of their effect upon one's own spiritual welfare, rather than upon other.* To be sure, such attitudes are sometimes viewed on the moral-social level and there construed as ideal ethical dispositions. But the classically Buddhist way to think of them is as contributing toward the individual spiritual advancement of the person who tries to perfect himself for Nirvana rather than as means to save the world.[5]

What this fails to explain, however, is the motivation of

[1]Edward Conze, *Buddhism: Its Essence and Development* (New York: Harper and Row, 1959), p. 39.

[2]*Ibid.,* p. 40.

[3]*Ibid.,* p. 40.

[4]*Ibid.,* p. 22.

[5]King, *Buddhism and Christianity,* pp. 81-82.

the Buddha. Having achieved Nirvana himself, why should he have devoted the next forty-five years of his life to the enlightening of others? To grasp the import of this question is to recognize the inadequacy of King's interpretation as well as to enter into the inwardness of Mahayana. It is of course not inaccurate to characterize Hinayana Buddhism as tending to be monastic. But it would be a totally false characterization of Mahayana. Buddhism is hardly the only religion to have known the polarity of the active and the contemplative life. The tension between the self and others, the individual and society, the world and God, the here-now and the beyond, in short, between the impulse to immediacy and the urge to transcendence is so central to human life that we should expect it to be reflected in all religions. Thus Christianity has had its own long bout with otherworldliness. It has asserted its kingdom to be not of this world and has advised rendering unto Caesar that which is Caesar's. It has barred the rich from the kingdom of heaven, and has exhorted its adherents to deny themselves and to let the dead bury the dead.

King is merely repeating the usual cliché about Budwhism when he asserts that

> Buddhism's depreciation of the worth and reality of human, space-time, physiocomental individuality has subtly undermined most expressions of human mutuality.[1]

> The fundamental root of man's misery is his existence as a personalized individual. (And for whatever form of Buddhism we survey, this holds true.) The "fall" of man, according to Buddhism, was his "fall" into individualized sentient being.[2]

> The physical renunciation of the princely life is consummated in the spiritual-mental quality of equanimity, a renunciation by detachment.[3]

These statements are distorted renderings of Buddhist teaching. More importantly, Christianity is also amenable

[1] *Ibid.*, p. 94.
[2] *Ibid.*, p. 115.
[3] *Ibid.*, p. 133.

to a construal which would open it to the same charges. Our task, however, is not to attempt to reverse King's subtle subversion of Buddhism in the interests of Christianity by doing the opposite. It is rather to point to the inwardness of oriental religiosity as against all external characterizations of it. And here this necessitates a few words apropos of the meaning of renunciation and detachment.

In what the Scriptures allege to be the first proclamation of his "teaching," namely in the Sermon at the Deer Park, the Buddha sets out the *Middle Way* as a course of life which avoids asceticism and mortification even as it shuns self-indulgence. In the light of this "teaching" all ascetic renderings of Buddhism misconceive its intent. The fundamental problem of human life is not man's "existence as a personalized being." It is rather how to deal with the ego which claims autonomy as against the whole of life. Whether it is a rich man's ego or a poor man's ego, whether it is the ego of a celibate or of a *bon vivant*, is for Buddhism not ultimately decisive. Hence the fundamental problem is not solved by a switch to celibacy, to poverty or to any other kind of mortification. To think otherwise, is for Buddhism to commit the mistake of the dog who bites the stick instead of the man wielding it. Enlightenment, therefore, is not a turning against life of the world, but the returning to life and the world of an ego which had been attempting to go it alone. Hence Hui Neng says, "to search for the Buddahood while separating from life is to search for a rabbit's horn." The meaning of this can never be understood by scholars determined to see Buddhism as an oriental variant of pessimism or stoicism.

Henri de Lubac, a French Catholic scholar, interprets Buddhist religious ideas in substantially the same manner as King. Perhaps his interpretation is even harsher than King's. In his *Aspects of Buddhism,* de Lubac maintains that the central core of Buddhism is to be found not in the nature of the Buddha but in his teaching. As proof, he quotes one of the Buddhist scriptures:

Of this great mass of material only a small proportion dates back to anywhere near the origin of the religion. There is nothing that in this respect resembles our New Testament; and so it is very difficult to recreate the earliest state of the doctrine, or to trace the early history of the religion, or even to know anything of a precise nature about the Buddha himself, although his historic existence and the main features of his moral personality are sufficiently well attested. This last point is, however, of little importance from the Buddhist point of view, for the empirical nature of the Buddha only plays a secondary part compared with the doctrine. "The Buddhas only point the way . . . the Law which I have given you will be your master when I disappear."[1]

While in one sense de Lubac's interpretation of the Buddhist concept of *dharma* is not to be faulted, he shows no awareness of its deeper meanings. It is true to say that the *dharma* is the essence of the Buddhist doctrine:

The Dharma is the Law or Doctrine. It consists in brief in the four "holy truths," the subject of the sermon of Benares. These are concerned with misery; the origin of misery; the suppression of misery; the way which leads to the suppression of misery.[2]

However, de Lubac ignores the non-duality of *dharma* and *buddha*. To Buddhists, *dharma* is not merely doctrine but fundamentally living truth. It is this living truth which is embodied by the Buddha himself. *Dharma* without Buddha becomes a general, abstract, objective doctrine, and Buddha without *dharma* becomes a merely charismatic individual with no ontological backing. In fact, the Buddha and the *dharma* are not to be separated from their social expression which is the *sangha* or the community. The three Jewels (*tri-ratna*) of Buddhism are Buddha, *dharma* and *sangha,* and the principle of non-duality obtains between all three, as also between the three bodies of the Buddha: the *dharmakaya, nirmanakaya,* and *sambhogakaya.*

[1] Henri de Lubac, *Aspects of Buddhism* (London: Sheed and War, 1953), pp. vi-vii.

[2] *Ibid.,* p. viii.

Henri de Lubac also sees Buddhism as pessimism. In his eyes, Buddhism teaches that man's redemption from misery is by way of the denial of man's existence. Redemption from misery—that is Nirvana—is a mystical experience. The idea of *nirvana,* according to de Lubac, is made out of an experience of ecstasy divorced from everyday life. Such ecstatic experience is to de Lubac not a mystical union of the divine and the human. Instead, it is a way of freeing the individual from this world. Thus he sees:

> Nevertheless, Buddhism does not believe in any substantial principle of individuality, nor in any substantial Absolute above or at the heart of the universe. And its general direction (at least in the early stages) is pragmatist; it is not a case of seeking for union with the Principle of the Universe but of escaping from the misery of this world, finding the "way out," and obtaining "deliverance." Hence the perpetually negative vocabulary.[1]

The Buddhist ideal is not this-wordly but other-worldly. By *other-worldly* de Lubac means advocating the renunciation of this world which is full of misery. This to de Lubac is the meaning of the middle way:

> The monastic ideal is an ideal of renunciation—of poverty and chastity; it is an ideal of the "middle way," of calm and inner freedom.[2]

To understand a religion in depth requires more than acquaintance with its formalities and their linguistic patterns. One must, for instance, understand the reason behind these linguistic usages before one can safely generalize about the religion. Buddhism—it is clear—has always avoided theistic language. Can we infer from this linguistic wariness that Buddhism has no concern with that reality which other religions point to by means of theistic language? Does Buddhism reject this reality or is it merely sensible of how far short of conveying this reality all language falls?

To say that the Buddhist merely wants to escape this

[1]*Ibid.,* p. x.
[2]*Ibid.,* p. vii.

world but does not seek to enter into or unite with higher reality is to confine Buddhist life to arbitrary limits. When he has escaped illusion, where shall one be if not in reality? Or does de Lubac envisage a third locus—a kind of limbo which is neither the heaven of reality nor the hell of illusion?

Of the spiritual meaning of the Middle Way, de Lubac evinces no awareness. It is not equatable with "the monastic idea of renunciation." How would de Lubac deal with the following statement: "Where there are no two extremes and therefore no need for a middle that is the true middle." In other words, Buddhism does not advocate renunciation as against acceptance of the world but rather union with the world in its ultimacy as well as in its immediacy in such a way that there is no dichotomy.

Henri de Lubac is also at pains to demonstrate the inferiority of Buddhist charity to Christian charity. He has some kind words for Buddhist charity. He sees it as consisting of loving-kindness (*maitri*), giving (*dana*) and compassion (*karuna*). His positive appraisal of Buddhist charity is expressed as follows:

> Maitri means a certain feeling, a certain state of mind, which is unassuming and gentle, but warm and friendly, and which should be habitually maintained. It is superior to any kind of practical activity; from it alone, in fact, does the latter derive any value it may possess.[1]

Such loving-kindness can be genuine, if it is related to the act of giving (*dana*). Perfect morality is made out of both inward feeling and outward action. And the act of giving with inward loving-kindness must also be inspired by compassion:

> It is all the more so as it does not find its fulfillment merely in any inward feeling, but has to be translated into action. Maitri is not genuine if it does not lead to dana (giving).[2]

> Dana is not therefore a superficial altruism. If it must al-

[1]*Ibid.*, p. 16.
[2]*Ibid.*, p. 20.

ways follow from maitri it must also be inspired more particularly by karuna (compassion, pity).[1]

This favorable interpretation of Buddhist charity is
gradually transformed into a purely objective presentation
of it in which one almost forgets whether de Lubac is prais-
ing it or criticizing it:

> No more than maitri is karuna (which specifies it) a purely
> negative state of mind. Nevertheless, it would be a mistake
> to imagine it as a sentimental attachment or a violent emo-
> tion. The man who knows may feel pity for those who do
> not know, but the more purified his pity becomes, the less
> he is moved by their sufferings; for, as we shall see later,
> the ultimate gain is an absolute indifference. It is a power
> which remains serene.[2]

He contrasts *maitri* with Christian charity as follows:

> Whatever may be the truth about the use of the word
> "Charity" as a translation of maitri or any other Buddhist
> word, in my opinion the identification of Buddhist charity
> with Christian charity even when made with certain reserva-
> tions, can only take place through misunderstanding, or, at
> least, a serious lack of analysis. Buddhism, even in its
> highest and most admirable forms, is entirely different in in-
> spiration from Christianity. It corresponds to a different
> idea. It has a different place, in a different scheme of salva-
> tion.[3]

The devaluation of Buddhist charity in the above quotation
becomes fully explicit in the following:

> Though there is every reason to believe that Sakyamuni
> himself—in so far as he can be discerned behind the mass
> of legend that grew up about him so long after his
> death—was a gentle, compassionate soul, full of loving-
> kindness and good works, it nevertheless remains true that
> the ideal of charity which developed in Buddhism grew out
> of beliefs which had absolutely no historical foundation at
> all. The Buddha, as he began to be depicted in his earlier

[1] *Ibid.*, p. 24.
[2] *Ibid.*, p. 25.
[3] *Ibid.*, pp. 31-32.

existences, and the Bodhisattvas, are purely legendary creatures.[1]

Moreover "this legendary character makes the ideal itself somewhat unreal and fantastic."[2] It makes Buddhism pessimistic in the sense that "the world which it creates is no more than a dream-world."[3]

> . . . on account of these very excesses the ideal forged by the Buddhist imagination ultimately becomes unrealisable.[4]
>
> The essential thing, the thing that puts a gulf between Buddhist charity and Christian charity, is that in Christianity the neighbour is loved for himself. In Buddhism that is impossible. It is true that in both religions charity consists, at least in its early stages, in loving the other for himself; but since in Buddhism the ego is entirely illusory, or exists only to be destroyed, it can hardly be loved for itself.[5]

The argument which de Lubac proffers is purely a priori. There is no evidence offered that de Lubac has made a comparative examination of a representative sample of Buddhist and Christian types and has found the latter to be in fact more loving of their neighbors than the former. By the manipulation of concepts of his own construing, he decides that in Buddhism it is impossible to love the neighbor for himself. If we are going to argue a prioristically, in fact, the reverse is true. Since Christianity sets a gulf between its absolute—the creator God—and creatures, to love a creature for itself is to insult the creator by absolutizing the creatures, that is, as stemming from their creator. In Buddhism, *per contra,* since there is no gulf set up between the absolute and the relative, the relative itself can be loved absolutely.

The living power of Buddhism cannot be appreciated, if one ignores the way in which Buddhism penetrated into the entire Far East. Its spread has been wholly peaceful and

[1]*Ibid.,* p. 32.
[2]*Ibid.,* p. 32.
[3]*Ibid.,* p. 33.
[4]*Ibid.,* p. 34.
[5]*Ibid.,* p. 37.

unlike Christianity, it has never allied itself with military power. Although it originated in India, it has been accepted by diverse people—Mongols, Indians, Chinese, Japanese, Tibetans, Burmese, Ceylonese, Vietnamese, Thailanders, Koreans, etc. It fertilized their cultures and entered into the patterns of daily life. How did a religion which is alleged to be pessimistic, escapist, lacking an ontological base, nihilistic and egoistic succeed in peacefully attracting such a diverse following and in persisting among them for two and a half millennia?

Thomas Altizer's interpretation of Buddhist religious ideas is partly conditioned by his own awareness of the limitations of the usual interpretation of them. He sees Buddhist religiosity both as antidotal to Christianity and as supplying the needed way out of the impasse of Christian theology today. His treatment of religion derives from a deep sense of the dialectical nature of the religious consciousness in which respect his is subtler than the approaches of King and de Lubac. He sees the opposition between Buddhism and Christianity as well as the possibility of a resolution of the contradictions. The resolution for him comes from the transcendence of both Christianity and Buddhism and points to a new Christian theology:

> First, we must disabuse ourselves of the priestly and ecclesiastical conviction that Christianity has already fully and finally revealed or unveiled itself. For in our turbulent and chaotic situation everything which we have been given as faith is crumbling in our midst, and we must either consign Christianity to a lost and increasingly forgotten past, or be prepared to accept the advent of a new Christianity which thus far has been theologically unrecognizable and unnameable.[1]

> Virtually all serious spokesmen for faith are now agreed that we are living in a new historical situation in which the traditional language of faith has become either archaic or

[1]Thomas Altizer, *The Descent into Hell* (Philadelphia: J. B. Lippincott Company, 1970), pp. 174-175.

unreal. Accordingly, the man of faith in our day is being driven to both an external and an internal silence.[1]

The discrepancy between traditional and contemporary consciousness, according to Altizer, is that between transcendence and immanence. Christianity is traditionally grounded on a faith in a transcendent creator, while the contemporary consciousness rejects any sort of transcendent being and would live by the light of immediacy.

The traditional belief that the divine is something which is other than ordinary reality, and that religious reality differs from what is actually immediately given in this world has been theologically formulated as the duality of creator and creature. On the contrary, contemporary consciousness tries to bridge this gulf and to soften or dissolve the duality. Traditional Christianity has not been friendly to any easing of the distinction of creature and creator, of transcendence and immanence, of the here-now and the beyond, etc.:

> But Christianity has never envisioned God as the All, for it has been unable to dissociate the name of God from a divine transcendence dividing the creature from the Creator.[2]

> Only Christianity knows the radical transcendence of God because only Christianity knows the finality of the Fall. It is the finality of the Fall which totally banishes the Christian from the immediate presence of the sacred, just as it is the reality of fallenness which seals the chasm between man and God and God and man.[3]

The dualistic understanding of traditional Christian theology has influenced occidental literature and philosophy:

> When an original sacred has wholly disappeared from view, then God is manifest not only as the Wholly Other, but also as the alien and empty God whose presence empties and alienates everything which it touches. This is that totally transcendent manifestation of God which Blake envisioned as Satan and Melville as Moby Dick, which Hegel

[1]*Ibid.*, p. 21.
[2]*Ibid.*, p. 178.
[3]*Ibid.*, p. 189.

conceived as abstract Spirit and Nietzsche named as the deification of nothingness.[1]

To deal with these difficulties of traditional faith, Altizer proposes an alternative to traditional Christian theology. His new proposal is based on a dialectical understanding of reality:

> Dialectical thinking and vision not only attempt to negate and transcend an established or given world of consciousness and society; they also attempt to annul or dissolve all those polarities and antinomies which alienate and isolate all individual centers of experience. Whether we turn to ancient or modern expressions of a dialectical way, we discover that it seeks out the lost or hidden ground of suffering and illusion.[2]

By the light of this dialectical methodology, Altizer seeks in oriental religion a way out of Christianity's difficulties:

> Inevitably, we ourselves will remain estranged from Christ and the Kingdom as long as we remain bound to what we have known as the transcendence of God. Moreover, we will remain bound to a divine transcendence so long as we understand transcendence as the eternal and primordial nature of God. Yet the Oriental vision can release us from such an understanding. For it confronts us with a vision of an original and primordial Totality which lies beyond what we have understood as the primordial nature of God. In the perspective of this vision, we can see that the West has never known a truly or fully primordial reality, has never known, at least in its Christian traditions, a primordial reality which is the original face or form of all reality whatsoever. Thus far it would seem that the Christian vision is necessarily a fallen vision: a vision apprehending both God and the world from the perspective of the Fall. It is what Christianity apprehends as the finality of the Fall which makes impossible for the Christian a full vision of an original innocence, just as it likewise closes the Christian to the possibility of a full and total vision of God. If nothing else, the Orient can teach us that Christianity has never em-

[1]*Ibid.*, p. 190.
[2]*Ibid.*, p. 10.

bodied a total vision, and thus the Christian has never truly or fully known God as a Totality or an All.[1]

It is the belief in the duality of the divine and the human which is responsible for man's alienation from reality. Believing that life should conform to the will of the divine, man finds himself unable to make it so. The immediate remains to a greater or lesser degree intractable to the full measure of transcendent demand placed upon it. This ineradicable contradiction between faith and practice forces the modern consciousness in its search for honesty into the rejection of the transcendental God, and to a reliance on immanent being. The modern consciousness has sought to free itself of its traditional allegiance to a transcendent reality and thereby to escape the schizophrenia which such a faith engenders:

> The mystery, the distance, the majesty, and the transcendence of God can here be understood as products of the Fall.[2]

> A divine transcendence is inseparable from its ground in an alienation and estrangement of man from God and man from man. Simply to affirm the impassable distance of God or the sacred realm is to sanction the brokenness of existence by accepting the eternal nature of an alienated world.[3]

> True, the Christian is alienated from the primordial bliss of an undifferentiated consciousness and alienated precisely because he has fallen into the actuality and activity of an isolated and differentiated consciousness.[4]

> Indeed, the classical forms of Western dualism have collapsed in the twentieth century, and collapsed because the chasm which we once knew between an inner and an outer realm has now become so great that all meaning of inner as inner and outer as outer has disappeared.[5]

[1] *Ibid.*, p. 177.
[2] *Ibid.*, p. 180.
[3] *Ibid.*, p. 181.
[4] *Ibid.*, p. 187.
[5] *Ibid.*, p. 198.

For Altizer, the fundamental weakness of traditional Christianity has been absolutization of the transcendent and its effort to force the human to submit to a reality beyond itself. Since human nature is resistant to this forcible subordination, Christianity has always excluded all forms of naturalism and this has rendered it vulnerable to subversion by the modern consciousness.

This being the fatal flaw of traditional theology, Altizer seeks a correction of it based on his understanding of Buddhism. To him, Buddhism is precisely concerned with what Christianity overlooks, for it stands neither for theological speculation about the divine transcendence nor for the humanistic affirmation of life of the individual, but for that total reality which is the non-duality of the human and the divine. Altizer seems to understand this, when he says:

> Who can doubt that the loss of God was an essential ground for the modern Western understanding of the Orient? For not only does the East know little or nothing of what the West has known as God, but the fullness of vision in the East precludes the possibility of the apprehension of deity. Or, at least, it negates every form of deity which stands isolated and enclosed within itself. Even Western words for faith and religion have been barriers to an understanding of the East, for here we have been initiated into a world of total vision which allows for no separation or division between a realm of the here and the now and the realm of the apart and the beyond. Simply to be open to Oriental vision is to be freed from the givenness and finality of Occidental religious forms and categories.[1]

The Buddhist vision of the fullness of reality to Altizer provides the needed antidote to Christian theology. Man's separateness can be annulled by the full vision of the All. There is no other way to heal the division set up by the Christian Fall:

> Wherever we turn in the higher expressions of Oriental religion, whether to Taoism, Hinduism, Buddhism, Jainism or Sankhya-Yoga, we find religious and mystical ways to an

[1]*Ibid.,* pp. 175-176.

original Totality. Not only does a full and total image of an
original Totality dominate the mystical ways of the East,
but these ways are themselves concrete paths to an original
and undifferentiated consciousness. Nothing comparable to
these Eastern ways of totally reversing all present and actual states of consciousness and experience is present in the
West, for Western religious ways, with the possible exception of the Kabbalah, have no way back to an original
All.[1]

Buddhism can lead us away from our dualistic understanding of love, an understanding sealing the fissure between
the within and the without and the chasm isolating the individual from the other.[2]

The sacred name of the Buddha is itself a total name or
image of the primordial Totality, and it draws into itself
every past reality or identity which it touches, thereby ab-
sorbing every past name or identity into itself.[3]

As far as Buddhism is concerned, it would seem unde-
niable that it is not subject to the weakness which Altizer
finds inherent in traditional Christian theology. The fact is,
however, that Altizer's rendering of Buddhism leaves it
open to the traditional charges leveled against it, to wit,
that it undermines individuality or at least is insufficiently
appreciative of it. In this regard, Altizer is still under the
influence of the basic occidental misunderstanding of oriental thought. The non-duality of the divine and the human
or of the self and the other, as the orient sees it, does not
call for a dissolution or erasure of man's individuality, actuality, experience, or desire. It is a distortion of Buddhism
to speak of it as Altizer does:

At no other point does Buddhism, and the Buddhist vision
of compassion, seem to be so relevant to our situation. For
if the full reality of the love which we have known now appears to us in the form of a negative totality, then Buddhism can be a way to the dissolution or erasure of that totality, to the absolute stilling of all active expressions of

[1]*Ibid.*, p. 185.
[2]*Ibid.*, p. 199.
[3]*Ibid.*, p. 204.

love or desire. If it is the activity and the temporality of a Western and Faustian will which have led to the horror and chaos of the twentieth century, then Buddhism offers a way to a stilling of that will, to an absolute silence and calm in which neither will nor desire will be present.[1]

Although he has some understanding of the Buddhist vision of the All, his understanding of non-duality is not in accord with the Buddhist conception.

Altizer is basically at one with Schopenhauer in holding that the Buddhist way to the primordial All is by the stilling of the will. Thus Altizer interprets Buddhist *nirvana* as the negation of life and of individual existence. As such it stands in opposition to its counterpart which is individual self-affirmation, and would seem to be vulnerable to the same criticisms which Altizer has leveled against the occidental concept of divinity. Thus he defines the Buddhist vision of *nirvana* as follows:

> The word "Nirvana" is derived from the Pali root *va*, "*to blow*." It designates a state in which the breath has ceased to move. Thus, it is common to understand Nirvana as meaning "blowing out." Stcherbatsky's masterly work on Nirvana maintains that its real meaning is the extinction of consciousness. Buddhists throughout the ages have described it as pure bliss. Yet it is a bliss that is absolutely beyond any experience or consciousness in which desire (*tanha*) is present, for Nirvana is the blowing out of desire, the final victory over pain and illusion. As the ultimate goal of the Buddhist quest, Nirvana can be achieved only when everything that is unreal (i.e., everything that is painful and transitory) within the disciple has been uprooted and destroyed. It demands the cessation not only of consciousness but of the whole man insofar as that man is affected by desire.[2]

Seen from Altizer's point of view, Buddhist Totality comes from the rejection of all particular existence and the negation of all the positive content of life in this actual world.

[1]*Ibid.*, p. 207.

[2]Altizer, *Oriental Mysticism and Biblical Eschatology* (Philadelphia: Westminster Press, 1961), p. 124.

In this respect, his understanding of Buddhism is both dualistic and pessimistic. The negation of all actual existence is for Altizer as for most occidental scholars also what is intended by *sunyata* which he alleges to mean "empty or void of reality."

On this interpretation, the Buddhist ultimate would be in violent opposition to the proximate and in the light of the ultimate the proximate must experience a devaluation. Thus Altizer's rendering of Buddhism reintroduces under another guise the dichotomy of transcendence and immanence which he is seeking to escape. Buddhism's own wrestlings with the problem of the relationship of *samsara* and *nirvana* should have taught him that the dualism is not so simply disposed of. The non-duality of *nirvana* and *samsara* which is the profoundest teaching of Mahayana is not attainable by the subordination of *samsara* to *nirvana* as transcendentalists would have it nor by the opposite subordination of *nirvana* to *samsara* as naturalists, humanists and the partisans of immediacy in general have sought it. Here then, Altizer departs from his dialectical methodology.

Altizer generally identifies the Primordial All with *nirvana:*

> Nirvana is one of a number of Oriental names and images for a total and primordial bliss.[1]

As equated with *nirvana* alone, the All would be exclusive of *samsara,* at times, however, Altizer proclaims Buddhist teaching to be the identity of *nirvana* and *samsara*. Thus, he approves Nagarjuna's dialectic:

> The most paradoxical position of Nagarjuna's positive dialectic is the identification of *samsara* and Nirvana.
>
> > We call this world Phenomenal;
> > But just the same is called Nirvana,
> > When from Causality abstracted.

[1]Altizer, *The Descent into Hell,* p. 193.

The Buddha has declared
That Ens and non-Ens should be both rejected.
Neither as Ens nor as non-Ens
Nirvana therefore is conceived.
If Nirvana were both Ens and non-Ens
Final deliverance would also both,
Reality and unreality together.
This never could be possible!
If Nirvana were both Ens and non-Ens,
Nirvana could not be uncaused.
Indeed the Ens and the non-Ens
Are both dependent on causation.

There is no difference at all
Between Nirvana and Samsara.
There is no difference at all
Between Samsara and Nirvana.
What makes the limit of Nirvana
Is also then the limit of Samsara.
Between the two we cannot find
The slightest shade of difference.[1]

Altizer also asserts the identity of *nirvana* and *samsara* in his discusion of the Buddhist dissolution of linguistic usages:

It is incapable of grasping the undifferentiated reality of *tathata*. It cannot reach to that still point where the dance of Nirvana and *samsara* takes place—where *samsara* and Nirvana are one.[2]

Nirvana is *samsara*; the world is a false or differentiated apprehension of the primal, undifferentiated Reality. In both Hinayana and Mahayana Buddhism, true Reality can be apprehended only by means of a mystical vision that is the product of the dissolution of man's normal mental and psychological states. But Hinayana Buddhism insists that such a vision can take place only through a radical turning away from the world, whereas Mahayana Buddhism grasps the world itself as Nirvana.[3]

Nirvana becomes present only through a realization of the

[1]Altizer, *Oriental Mysticism and Biblical Eschatology*, pp. 139-40.
[2]*Ibid.*, p. 151.
[3]*Ibid.*, p. 175.

nothingness of the world. Ultimately, the world qua world is empty of reality in so far as Nirvana is all reality whatsoever. Nirvana is *samsara*: *samsara* is Nirvana. Ontologically, there is no distinction between reality and illusion, Nirvana and the world, or the Bodhisattva and the sinner. Just as there is no Self, there is no world, there is no pain, and there is no illusion. Accordingly, compassion is an individual openness to the unreality of differentiated things and the reality of an undifferentiated Nirvana.[1]

Two qualifications need to be noted. First of all Buddhism does not assert the identity of *nirvana* and *samsara* but their non-duality. Secondly, on the level on which there is no pair, no world, and no illusion, there is also no *Bodhisattva,* no compassion, no openness and nothing to be open to. Hence to describe compassion as "individual openness to the unreality of differentiated things and the reality of an undifferentiated Nirvana" is to wholly misconstrue Buddhist teaching even as it puts *nirvana* on a higher level than *samsara.*

Altizer's understanding of identity of *samsara* and *nirvana* vacillates between the Buddhist way of understanding it and a quasi-Christian eschatological way of understanding the matter. He frequently sees it as calling for an ultimate dissolution of this worldly reality and thus the identity of *samsara* and *nirvana* is not an identity of the profane reality and the sacred reality but that of *samsara* as unreality and *nirvana* as void of all worldly reality. It is precisely because *samsara* is ultimately nothing that Altizer holds it to be one with *nirvana* which is also an absolute void:

But from the point of view of faith, all human creativity, all existence as being, all truth, and all consciousness, is grounded in sin, suffering, and death. For the believer must yearn for that Day when God will be all in all. He must know that Reality in which Nirvana is *samsara* and *samsara* is Nirvana. He must live in that Reality in which

[1]*Ibid.,* pp. 183-184.

being has come to an End, in which love has made all
things one, in which pain and death are no more.[1]

We can see its counterpart in Buddhism's absolute negation of the illusion and pain of *samsara* as the hither side
of its total affirmation of Nirvana.[2]

The vow of the Bodhisattva, to remain at the brink until all
enter Nirvana before him, amounts to a vow to remain as
he is forever. This vow symbolizes the Buddhist truth, as
Heinrich Zimmer has noted, that *samsara* and Nirvana do
not exist as opposition, for both are equally emptiness
(*sunyata*), the Void.[3]

Seen from this point of view, the non-duality of *samsara*
and *nirvana* is the void of *samsara* and *nirvana*. In other
words, the non-duality of them is not to be taken as, for example, that of a natural thing (a stone) and divine being
(its creator) but to that of the unreality of a stone and the
unreality of a creator. Thus the identity must be made
through the absolute Void. According to Altizer, the doctrine of Void plays this important role in Buddhist thought.
It is the basis for Buddhist religious reality. Anything which
is opposed to the Void is considered as being unreal religiously. In a nutshell, *samsara* can be identified with
nirvana only when it is ultimately negated. Buddhist med-
itation is directed towards this negation:

> Buddhist meditation is directed to the dissolution of the
> world and the self as *samsara*; so likewise the Christian life
> treats the world (the Old Aeon) with absolute indifference,
> and the Christian life is possible only through a deep aware-
> ness of the underlying unreality of the world.[4]

There is no doubt that Christian *Contemptus Mundi* is
an attitude founded on dualism and oriented towards a
kingdom not of this world. Altizer radically confuses things
in pairing this attitude with the Buddhist claim of the non-

---

[1] *Ibid.,* p. 194.
[2] Altizer, *The Descent into Hell,* p. 55.
[3] *Ibid.,* p. 195.
[4] Altizer, *Oriental Mysticism and Biblical Eschatology,* p. 178.

duality of *nirvana* and *samsara* and makes of the religious life a special mystical ecstasy divorced from normal life.

> Despite its dialectical foundations, the Madhyamika is obviously a philosophical expression of mystical experience and intuition. At this time in Indian religious history the deeper practices of concentration were producing an ecstatic "reversal" that transformed the world itself into ultimate Reality. The Vedantic school of Hinduism illustrates this process, but most scholars believe that it arose after and was even, influenced by the Madhyamika. Thomas notes that "in the long-prepared ecstasy the saint has beheld and grasped the all-unity, and although he awakes again to normal life, i.e., is again brought back to distinction of subject and object, perceives colors, sounds, etc., feels feelings, and thinks thoughts, yet his consciousness of reality is fundamentally transformed by his post-ecstatic retrospection, just in this sense that now everything actual appears empty and unreal, dreamlike and illusory." In this vision, *samsara* is grasped as being unreal—and with it the process of transmigration itself.[1]

When Buddhism is reduced to concepts and doctrine, as it almost inevitably is in the hands of scholars, only self-contradiction ensues. Reality is not grasped by ecstasy and both ecstasy and post-ecstatic retrospection are *samsara* states. Buddhism does not open its depths to the subtlest scholarship or the most acute intellectuality and that is all that scholarship can bring to the task.

Altizer is also of the opinion that *nirvana* and *sunyata* constitute the basis of Buddhist ethics. To him, compassion is possible only when individuality is negated. Love is possible only because one's ego is insignificant and nothing. In other words, Altizer sees the self is worthy of giving away because it is not worthy of having. In this way, Altizer sees *nirvana* and *sunyata* as fundamental for Buddhist ethics:

> Paradoxical as it may appear to the Western mind, emptiness and compassion are inextricably associated in Buddhism. When everything is known to be empty of "real-

[1]*Ibid.,* p. 139.

ity,'' then radical self-giving can become not only a possibility but rather a necessity of genuine or true existence. It is precisely because the self is unreal that it can be given to the other; it is precisely because all things are ultimately identical that compassion is the most authentic response to the true nature of reality. At bottom the doctrine of the Void is the Buddhist means of identifying love as the center of reality, a center which here becomes all in all. Finally, Buddhism itself dissolves in response to the ultimate and universal reality of love. For if nothing separates the realm of suffering and illusion from the goal of release, then there is no way from ignorance and entanglement to enlightenment and freedom. Not only is there no way to enlightenment or Nirvana, but there is no Enlightened One, no Buddha. Buddhism ultimately demands the destruction of all words, the dissolution of all concepts.[1]

Its negative apprehension of all things as empty or void (*sunya*) of reality is at bottom a positive way of realizing all things as ultimate reality or Nirvana itself. So it is that Mahayana Buddhism proclaims and practices compassion (*karuna*) as the primary reflection of the Void. For a true realization of the ultimate identity of all beings necessarily results in a practice of total compassion.[2]

Altizer presents *sunyata* as being transcendent to existence postulated by thought and as identical with existence postulated by intuition:

The Real is transcendent to thought; it is nondual (*sunya*), free from the duality of ''is'' and ''not-is.'' Indeed, the categories of ''is'' and ''not-is'' are products of conceptual thought, and thus are exposed as being contradictory and unreal. Consequently, one can say neither that the *dharmas* exist nor that they do not exist. No conceptual statement about reality is admissible. Existence as a category can only be postulated by intuition and not by thought. (Here one can see how this highest system of Indian mysticism parallels the modern empirical-scientific epistemologies of the West.)[3]

[1]Altizer, *The Descent into Hell*, pp. 195-196.
[2]*Ibid.*, p. 194.
[3]Altizer, *Oriental Mysticism and Biblical Eschatology*, pp. 138-139.

His interpretation of *sunya* has some validity in the sense that it is not merely emptiness of reality but emptiness of objective, abstract, and rational knowledge which engenders the duality between being and non-being. However, the non-duality of being and non-being is never by Altizer fully connected with the non-duality of seeker and sought. The central meaning of *sunyata* is not merely nondual concept but nondual reality which is human, natural and at the same time divine. It has to be something which is inseparably rooted in each individual life. And thus it is surely related to everything including thought. The religious reality is not transcendent to thought, but it makes thought alive. In other words, it makes words alive, and makes the word ring true. As soon as the word has the very truth, it is no longer mere word but Word which is existentially married with man's whole being. Otherwise stated, language and concept are not rejected; Buddhism only insists that our words shall be Words and our thoughts Thoughts.

As a result of his misconception of Buddhist nonduality of *sunyata,* he also misunderstands Buddhist love when he says:

> All the higher expressions of Oriental vision, culminate in a realization of the One or the All, and total compassion is the Buddhist embodiment of that All. But Buddhist love can never truly be named or understood: It can only be immediately realized in a total point or moment which must appear to an alien vision as a void or nothingness.[1]

> Pity can be a genuine expression of Buddhist compassion because a total expression of pity can effect a full identification with another.[2]

> Only an actual obliteration of that estrangement can be given the name of compassion, an obliteration which actually negates the reality of estrangement.[3]

He does not conceive of love as non-duality of the reality of the world and the reality of the sacred:

[1]Altizer, *The Descent into Hell,* p. 196.
[2]*Ibid.,* p. 202.
[3]*Ibid.,* p. 202.

Only a religious vision that can dissolve the claims of the "reality" of the world can give birth to a higher and sacrificial vision of love.[1]

Another misperception of Buddhist love is expressed in his understanding of non-duality of self and other. According to him, non-duality of self and other is unreality of self and other. To Buddhists, however, there can be no real love when there are no real individuals. Human relationships can never be truly real unless the self as well as the other is real. How can unreality of self and other engender real love? To Buddhists, the non-duality of self and other means the true relatedness of self and other. Losing self or denying self means passing from a life characterized by unrelatedness to a life of relatedness. The deepest meaning of denying self is not the substitution of a selfless state of life, but the finding of true self in the relatedness of self and other. This true self comes no more from denying individuality than from affirming it. In other words, self becomes not unreal but increasingly real only when it involves itself in really real relatedness. The true lesson of Buddhism is neither to deny life nor to affirm life, but to find the true self in the nonduality of self and other. In this way, the other will no longer stand against self, and vice versa. Relatedness is neither a surrendering of the self to an other, nor a conquering of the other. In every aspect of human life, individuality has to have its place. The ultimate and universal reality of life, without the immediate and particular reality of love, is merely an abstraction. Altizer misses the deeper sense of the non-duality of self and other, when he says:

So long as we understand love as mutual and integral relationship between two isolated centers of consciousness and experience, then we shall remain closed to the advent of a new consciousness and experience which negates and transcends all such isolated and individual centers. So long as we attempt to practice compassion as an individual re-

[1]Altizer, *Oriental Mysticism and Biblical Eschatology*, pp. 149-150.

sponse to the unique and individual feeling of another—
whether that group be an isolated individual or distinct and
individual group—we shall be closed to the advent of a new
form of the other, a form in which individual identity, as
we have known it, will have been negated and transcended.
Buddhism can lead us away from our dualistic understanding of love, an understanding sealing the fissure between
the within and the without and the chasm isolating the individual from the other.[1]

The persistence of a dualistic mode of thought in Altizer despite his intentions is abundantly evident. The distinctions
he draws between religious reality and the profane reality,
and between this-worldly reality and other-worldly reality
keep him from understanding the non-duality of self and
other as Buddhists conceive of it. According to his point of
view, religious reality is not rooted in man's individual existence. Whatever else religious reality may be, it must be
that which is ontologically related to human individuality.
Religious reality cannot be the outcome of a radical denial
of everyday life, nor can it be the outcome of radical affirmation of it. Nor can it be the outcome of dialectical virtuosity, but only of existential living. As soon as religious reality is existentially grasped, it is already inseparable from
personal life. And this is exactly what the Buddha attained
in his life. He attained it by putting his whole life into it,
not by making intellectual distinctions. When one thinks of
the Buddha's agonizing quest for reality there is something
very obscene as well as very comical in a scholar's attempt
to gain the Buddha's victory by a conceptual clarification
such as the following:

Three different meanings of the word occur throughout the
book. First, "reality" will designate the meaning of the
real in the profane (or this-worldly) consciousness, which
here includes scientific, practical, and Western philosophical understanding. Then, the term Reality is employed to
point to the meaning of the real in the religious consciousness (which here comprehends the religious, the sacred,

[1]Altizer, *The Descent into Hell*, p. 199.

and the transcendent realms). Finally, reality in a neutral sense will simply designate the real, without any reference to its ultimate evaluation. Obviously, this punctuation exposes the bias of the author—who is committed to the religious Reality.[1]

In any case, this is the point at which to record the author's deepest intellectual debt, and that is to Joachim Wach for his idea of the ultimate Reality. Under this heading can be fitted the Christian God, the Buddhist Nirvana, the Chinese Tao, the Hindu Brahman-Atman, etc. The author differs from Professor Wach in believing that this Reality is wholly other than the reality of Being; therefore he calls it the religious Reality.[2]

Altizer's dualistic reading of Buddhist religious thought is expressed also in the very contrast he draws between Buddhism and Christianity. To him, Buddhism is a way of going back to the Primordial All, while Christianity is a way of going forward to the eschatological All:

The one is a negation and a forward-moving transcendence of a given form of consciousness and identity, whereas the other is a negation and a backward-moving reversal of the movement and activity of consciousness. Christian compassion is an actual and real transformation of consciousness and selfhood, whereas Buddhist compassion is a dissolution and annihilation of selfhood, and self-consciousness. Therefore Christian compassion totally reverses the pity and compassion of the Buddha, even if this reversal is a dialectical reversal, a reversal embodying the "emptiness" of Buddhist compassion in the actuality of time and flesh.[3]

Here Altizer posits himself as a Christian theologian and thus his "position" is not existential. In other words, he sees himself as *what* he is rather than as *who* he is. Buddhism, as Buddhists conceive of it, is not a dialectical counterpart to Christian religion. Buddhist thought in itself is complete and is not in need of the other. Buddhism as living truth, that is, not as philosophical or theological

[1]Altizer, *Oriental Mysticism and Biblical Eschatology*, p. 10.
[2]*Ibid.*, p. 13.
[3]Altizer, *The Descent into Hell*, p. 203.

truth, is neither dialectical nor conceptual. For it, the problem is not whether to go backward or forward but how to get *into* life. Its living truth is neither silence nor speech; it neither goes backward nor forward; it upholds neither negating nor affirming, neither atheism nor theism, neither primordial nor eschatological. The Buddhist way is not directed towards the horizontal realm nor does it aspire to the vertical realm. Buddhist reality is a truth to be lived. Life in its inmost nature cannot be posited, for it is unlimited. As soon as it is posited by man, it becomes something exclusive. Every position has its opposition. Buddhism as religious life is no position, and there is nothing in it to be changed or reversed.

The essential thrust of Buddhist religious thought is toward life itself. The proper study of Buddhism is not to compare or contrast its linguistic usages or historically conditioned events with the other but to reenter into the life of life, the ontological source of all lives. Re-entry into life is conditioned by neither owning nor disowning, neither rejecting nor accepting, neither negating nor affirming. Nonduality is not the kind of void of which Altizer envisages it to be. Rather it is ontological relatedness without which there is no thing whatsoever. Life itself is no closer to the divine than it is to the natural and to the human. At the same time, it is as close to the divine as it is to the natural and the human. In other words, it is inseparable from the natural and the human and the divine. This is the central meaning of fundamental Buddhist concepts such as *buddhahood, sunyata, nirvana,* or *karuna.*

It must be made clear that the ontological relatedness does not exclude any reality whatsoever. It is not a product of any particular man or religion. It is not a thing and yet it is not opposed to anything. To know ontological relatedness is to live it. To live it is to be whole. It is the meaning of ontological relatedness that it is not divorced from life, and thus it is inseparable from man's individual life. Only man's personal life can be holy, that is,

whole. Buddhism as living reality is the restoration of man
to himself, to nature and to the divine.

In conclusion, then, it is clear that Altizer's deepest intellectual understanding of religion is dualistic in the sense
that religious reality is something which is different from
other realities. And thus, he misunderstands Buddhist religiosity which is separable neither from the profane nor
from the sacred. Nor is Buddhist religiosity simply the unreality of the profane and the sacred. On the contrary, it is
the nonduality of the profane and sacred, or in other
words, religious reality is inseparable from the whole human being. Buddhist non-duality is not a betweenness
which occurs between two existences. Rather non-duality is
a lived or existential ontology in which the human, the divine and the natural are wholly one. Since man in his nature is not merely human but also natural, the wholeness
of man must be wholly natural and wholly human. And the
non-duality of the natural and the human is one's true self
which cannot be objectively known, for what is objective is
separated from oneself. Man's true self therefore cannot be
limited to this or that, and in this sense the true self is infinite and is ontologically related to the divine. That is why
religious reality in the Buddhist sense of the word cannot
be opposed to any other reality whatsoever.

Seen from this point of view, Buddhist religiosity,
whether it is expressed in the Buddha's silence or his
smile, in *nirvana,* or in *sunyata,* does not point to an unbridgeable gulf between the divine and the human, or between the human and the natural, but to the inseparable relatedness of the divine and the human and of the human
and the natural. In this respect, Buddhist religiosity is
neither theological nor philosophical nor dialectical.

CHAPTER V

CHINESE RELIGIONS AND THE
RELIGION OF CHINA

Apart from the less than ten percent of the Chinese population who followed either Islam or Christianity, the majority of the rest until recently followed the *san chiao* or the three religions—Confucianism, Taoism, and Buddhism. Chinese culture over the past two millennia has incorporated the influence of all three, and each of the three shows the influences of the other two. Confucianism and Taoism are indigenous crystallizations out of the matrix of Chinese primitivism. Buddhism was an imported religion but was thoroughly domesticated and suffused with the Chinese spirit. Thus Buddhism entered China not as a displacer of what was already there but as a partner in an enlarged enterprise. Chinese religious openness in this respect is without parallel in the history of the major religions. Buddhism for its part readily accommodated itself to Chinese ways. Both Buddhist adaptability and Chinese openness typify the spirit of oriental religious culture.

With the aim of harmony and relatedness, the Chinese attempt to embrace the truth of another rather than to fight it. Of course, Chinese history is not without its periods of persecution of religion. Nevertheless, the issues themselves were not religious but political, economic or sociological. The spirit of Chinese religiosity must be sought not only in the particular religions themselves but as much in the relatedness of the three. It is in the spirit of relatedness that the fundamental ways of the three religions are one and the same. The deepest Chinese feeling in the matter is that each of the *san chiao* is complete in itself, that each points to the same ultimate goal, that the goal may be reached along the path prescribed by each and that nonetheless each is in need of as well as supplementary of the other two.

Where this is not understood, scholars will see Confucian religious ideas as opposed to Taoist religious ideas. As a result, they will tend to interpret Confucian religious ideas as being merely ethical, even as they will be likely to regard Taoist religious ideas as being merely quietistic. They will separate the Confucian *tao* from the Taoistic *tao* and see both as sundered from Buddhist *sunyata*.

The Chinese view of ultimate truth is that it cannot be one-sided. It is never *this* as opposed to *that*. Absolute truth is not in opposition to anything, and wherever one position is set over its opposite we are dealing only with partial truths which are to be encompassed in a higher truth. This sense of religious truth is not exclusive but inclusive; it is not dualistic but non-dualistic. Because their approaches are so markedly conditioned by dualistic modes of thought, scholars who are otherwise deeply sympathetic towards Chinese religious culture fail to penetrate its essential inwardness.

Martin Buber is one of the most influential apostles of existential awareness as well as the best-known Jewish religious thinker in the twentieth century. He was greatly interested in understanding oriental religious ideas for the development of his own thought-pattern, and has dealt with Chinese thought in some of his early writings. His "China and Us"[1] presents his interpretation of Confucianism, while "The Teaching of the Tao"[2] does the same for Tao-

[1]Martin Buber, "China and Us," in *A Believing Humanism* (New York: Simon and Schuster, 1967). This is an address at the Fall, 1928, conference of the China Institute, Frankfurt-am-Main, Germany. Its original title is *China und Wir*.

[2]It is an introduction to his 1909 translation of *Talks and Parables of Chuang-tzu* (Reden und Gleichnisse des Tschuang-Tze), Leipsig: Insel-Verlag, 1910.

ism. His evaluation of Zen Buddhist thought may be found in "The Place of Hasidism in the History of Religion"[1] which was written somewhat later.

Buber's early thought-pattern differs from his later one in that his early thought is "mystical" in a sense which he later rejected, namely in the sense of denying the ultimacy of individuality. His later thought development is based on the dialogical principle expounded in his *I and Thou*. This dialogical principle, he claims, transcends mysticism without rejecting it. In other words, his fully developed thought-pattern may perhaps be viewed as a combination of Kierkegaard's mystical relationship between man and God and Feuerbach's humanistic relationship between man and man. In his early thought, he later felt that he had ignored the importance of individuality, while his later thought strives to give due recognition to it. It can in a way be said that his early thought is more Platonic and his later thought is more Aristotelian.

Buber's later thought-patterns are rooted in his philosophical outlook on man. While he shows some sympathy to Zen thought so far as it is akin to Hasidic thought, his handling of oriental religious thought in general is critical.

His dialogical principle in its nature is based on the twofold movement of speaking and of hearing. It presupposes distance as well as relation. There is sharing, mutuality, participation, but also separateness, hence duality and no final merging. Duality is the presupposition of dialogue. This duality in fact influences his critique of oriental religious ideas. The period of his interest in Confucianist and Taoist religious ideas precedes the period of his writing on Zen thought. His early thought issued in a mysticism in which there was no sharing, no mutuality, no participation, and no duality of individual and God. Thus his early mysti-

[1] Its original title is *Der Ort des Chassidismus in der Religionsgeschichte*. It is found in *Die Chassidische Botschaft* (Heidelberg: Verlag Lambert Schneider, 1943). It is translated as *Hasidism* in English (New York: Philosophical Library, Inc. 1948).

cism does not allow dialogue between man and the ultimate. Mysticism thus he understood as meaning man's oneness with God without any relationship between man and man. Later he came to hold that the ultimate relationship both between man and man and between man and God is dialogical and hence as preserving as well as presupposing the separateness of the individual involvement. For Buber as for Schweitzer, religion is also a field of action, and it is on this score that he finds Judaism especially praiseworthy. The spiritual quest of the Jewish religion has always emphasized the deed:

> It is Judaism's basic tenet that the deed as an act of decision is an absolute value.[1]

All the Semitic religions emphasize man's activity in comparison with other religions and among the Semitic religions Judaism is supreme in this regard:

> Of all the spiritual creations of mankind, Judaism alone endows man's decision with such centrality in all that comes to pass, and such meaningfulness.[2]

Furthermore, he argues that oriental spirituality can attain integral religiosity only when they are associated with Judaic emphasis on man's deed:

> Through the fervor of its demand for return, and the fervor of its belief in the power and the glory of return, through its new magic, the magic of decision, Judaism won the Occident for the teaching of the Orient. By means of this teaching Judaism became the representative of the Orient at its best.[3]

In other words, Buber believes that the secret of "authentic life" lies in Judaic religiosity:

> Of the great spiritual systems of the Orient, the one destined to have a decisive effect on Occidental man had to be the system whose proclamation of the way of authentic

[1]Martin Buber, On Judaism (New York: Schocken Books, 1967), p. 67.
[2]Ibid., p. 67.
[3]Ibid., p. 68.

life challenged every individual directly, the system that
was not the privilege of the sage or the chosen but equally
accessible to all, and that appealed especially and most
powerfully to the man who has lost his way or who lacked
direction, to the "sinner": the Jewish teaching of decision
and return. Other teachings influenced the sages and the
chosen; the Jewish teaching influenced the nations, the people of the West.[1]

Oriental religion without the Judaic insight is apt to be a-
historical, non-ethical, and abstract. To Buber, man's self-
realization or his enlightenment is not so important, because for him these are void of activity. Insight, realization, attainment, or enlightenment of the Far Eastern religions he considers the opposite of constant effort and
achievement. To Buber, the life of human relationship is
not based on contemplation; it is grounded in man's activity.

His examination of Confucian religious ideas was at
least in part practically motivated:

Is there something that we can receive from living Chinese
reality, from the real life powers of its customs, its education, its culture, and if so what?[2]

He answers his own question in the negative:

It does not seem to me now that there is anything that we
can take over in this sense from the Confucian culture.[3]

The reason for his negative conclusion is that its presuppositions are fundamentally alien to occidental man. For
Buber, the foundations of Confucianism rest on ancestor
worship and on an image of original man. The ancestor
cult expresses the basic Confucian attitude towards the
dead which for Buber means the possibility of natural com-
munion with the dead. Buber avows that it is through this
relationship with the dead the Chinese receive the ultimate
principle of life. Natural as it may be to the Chinese, inter-

[1]Ibid., p. 69.
[2]Buber, "China and Us," p. 187.
[3]Ibid., p. 187.

course with the dead is an utterly strange phenomenon to the occident:

> The foundations of this ancestor cult are not given in the West.[1]

Buber also finds in Confucianism a longing to return to the original man. This original man, the "pure man of yore," Buber takes to be man in the primordial state, man in the paradisiacal primal state, or the original Man (Adam). The original man can be identified with the sinless man. According to Buber, Confucianism is based on the belief in such a primal paradise. To return to the golden age, the primordial state, or the paradisiacal condition of mankind is taken to be the Confucian ideal for both man and the state. But again, Buber claims that such an ideal is impossible for the occident, because only the fallen state is present in occidental consciousness:

> This trust in the primal being is missing in the Western man and cannot be acquired by him. Even Christianity was not able to alter this situation, although it did, in fact, transmit to the West the Oriental teaching of the paradisiacal primal state of mankind. Of the biblical story of the first man, only the fall is present in a living way in the reality of the personal life of Christian Western man, not the life before the fall.[2]

Thus neither of the pillars on which Confucianism rests—neither its cult of ancestors nor its ideal of return to primal man—can serve as supports for the religious consciousness of occidental man.

Both the ancestor cult and the belief in sinless man are impossible and foreign to the occident, because these Confucian beliefs seemed to Buber to be excessively supernatural. Chinese concern with the dead as well as the ideal of a sinless state both transcend man's daily life and are thus unable to seriously interest the contemporary occidental.

The Chinese scholar, Hu Shih, interprets Confucianism

[1]*Ibid.,* p. 188.
[2]*Ibid.,* p. 189.

in a quite opposite way. According to Hu Shih, Confucianism is not primarily an ancestor cult but rather a teaching of filial piety in this life:

> And the Confucianists actually tried to found a new religion of filial piety without the benefit of the gods. This religion centers around the idea that the human body is the sacred inheritance from the parents, and must always be regarded as such. "There are three forms of filial piety: the highest is to glorify one's parents; next, not to degrade them; and lastly, to support them." "This body is inherited from our parents. How dare we act irreverently with this inheritance? Therefore, to live carelessly is a sin against filial duty; so is disloyalty to our princes; so is dishonesty in office; so is faithlessness to friends; and so is lack of courage on the battlefield. Failure in any one of these five duties will disgrace one's parents. Dare we act without reverence?" "The dutiful son never moves a step without thinking of his parents; nor utters a word without thinking of his parents." The parents thus take the place of God or the gods - as a new moral sanction of human action.[1]

Confucianism for Hu Shih is a naturalistic religion. He sees it as theologically agnostic and as ethically humanistic:

> Confucius was a humanist and an agnostic. When asked about death and the proper duties to the spirits and the gods, he replied: "We know not about life, how can we know death? And we have not learned how to serve men, how can we serve the gods?" Life and human society are the chief concern of the Chinese people. Confucius also said: "To say that you know a thing when you know it, and to say that you do not know when you know it not, that is knowledge." That is his formulation of agnosticism.[2]

Hu Shih's interpretation of Confucianism is close to Lin Yutang's:

[1]Hu Shih, *The Chinese Renaissance* (Chicago: The University of Chicago Press, 1934), p. 82.

[2]*Ibid.*, p. 81.

For Confucianism is the religion of the "gentleman," of "good breeding" and "good manners."[1]

Hu Shih's interpretation of Confucianism as an ethical humanism makes of it something not out of line with Buber's interpretation of Judaism. If Hu Shih is right, both are based on the deed:

> The great sages of ancient China were men of ceaseless active life. It was said of Confucius that "he knew it impossible, but he would endeavour to do it." And Mo Ti, the founder of the *Mo* school of philosophy, travelled from state to state in his tireless effort to preach his ideas of universal love and international peace. Courage was one of the three cardinal virtues of Confucianism. Progress was a generally accepted principle of social and political thinking of the third and second centuries B.C. Any one who read the philosophical writings of ancient China, notably those of Han Fei and the Hsün Tse, will know that progress, reform and even the active conquest of nature were their common ideals.[2]

While Hu Shih's ethico-humanistic interpretation of Confucianism has its own measure of truth, it does not touch the heart of the matter any more than does Buber's. Hu Shih is surely right in claiming that Confucianism has a strong ethical component and thus relevant to contemporary occidental consciousness. Seen from Hu Shih's perspective, Confucius is not concerned with the past as past or with returning to the past. He is not seeking a *return to* original man but an entry into true manhood here and now and thus he is concerned with the present life. Referring to the past, Confucius wanted to use it to revitalize the present life:

> The Master said, He who by reanimating the Old can gain knowledge of the New is fit to be a teacher.[3]

[1] Lin Yutang, *From Pagan to Christian* (New York: Avon Book Division, 1959), p. 56.
[2] Hu Shih and Lin Yu-Tang, *China's Own Critics* (New York: Paragon Book Reprint Corp., 1969), p. 72.
[3] *Analects,* 2:11, as translated in Waley, *Analects,* p. 90.

Confucius is fundamentally a teacher of men. His teaching activity is not separable from that which he seeks to convey, and neither the content nor the method of his teaching is separable from his own being. His teaching and his life are one. In this sense, his way, his truth and his life are one. His was not a teaching to be objectively appropriated. As a truly creative and existential teacher he neither imposes his own idea upon others nor presents purely objective data about the past. Creative teaching comes into being only when a teacher relates himself to his task with his whole being, and for this he must be in touch with his whole being. Man as a whole being is the goal or source of Confucianism and this wholeness is not simply psychological but cosmic:

> The Master said, Heaven begat the power (*te*) that is in me. What have I to fear from such a one as Huan T'ui?[1]

> If Heaven does not intend to destroy such culture, what have I to fear from the people of K'uang?[2]

> The Master said, He who has put himself in the wrong with Heaven has no means to expiation left.[3]

Neither Buber nor Hu Shih show any understanding of the ontological basis of Confucian religious ideas. As a result, Hu Shih's interpretation limits Confucianism to ethical culture, while Buber's sees him as impossibly supernaturalistic.

Confucius' religious thought is centered around the quest for true manhood and this necessitates going beyond psychology and ethics to man's ultimate ground. Confucian religious reality can be encountered neither by the self-forgetful performance of ancestral rites nor by ethical endeavor alone since these by themselves do not summon up man's total being.

In the cardinal concept of Confucianism, *jen,* one can find the central thrust of Confucian religious thought. *Jen*

[1]*Ibid.,* 7:22.
[2]*Ibid.,* 9:5.
[3]*Ibid.,* 3:13.

indicates neither a possessed life nor a free life. To Confucianists, it is the source of all existential truth.

It is seen as the gem of life: it is life itself.[1] Confucius is depicted as follows:

> He devotes himself to the realization of a religion of ethics, the consecration of Man to Man. *To him, humanity is God, the Harmony of life his ultimate.*[2]

If it is truly life itself, there is no other living truth or reality apart from *jen*. The man who lives *jen* is called a true man or a sage. A sage, however, does not stand in opposition to an ordinary man. On the contrary, a sage relates himself to his parents, his wife, his children, his brother and sister, his friend, and his employer. These relationships are for him truthful, that is filled with truth and reality, and in and through these relations, he encounters the ultimate truth and reality of life. Confucianism is religion not in the sense that it proclaims the existence of supernatural entities but in its quest for an absolute relation to life itself. In such human relationships, the individual is always supported by Heaven. In fact, his relation with others is not distinguishable from his relation with Heaven. Buber strangely does not see Confucius as having the same deep concern in himself with achieving true relatedness between men, with being, "a man among other men?" [3] Buber's criticism is purely superficial, and it is not apparent that he entered into a living relationship with Confucian religious thought.

Leaving to one side that which is abstract, Confucius is concerned with human life as lived. What is apart from life is for Confucius as for Buddha abstract. In *jen,* that is, in life, all reality becomes alive. And thus truth in association with *jen* is neither scientific nor metaphysical, but existen-

[1]Francis C. M. Wei, *The Spirit of Chinese Culture* (New York: Charles Scribner's Sons, 1947), p. 60.

[2]Kakasu Okakura, *The Ideals of the East* (New York: E. P. Dutton and Company, 1903), p. 27.

[3]See *Analects,* 18:6, as translated in Waley, *The Analects of Confucius,* p. 220. "If I am not to be a man among other men, then what am I to be?"

tial. *Jen* is existential in the sense that it is inseparable from man's personal life. For example, truth can be really true only when a man is true. Reality, apart from a man's being real, is to Confucius an abstraction, and thus dead. By the same token, an ideal, which cannot be actualized, is neither true nor ultimate. Seen from this point of view, God as separate from man can be likened to a "ghost in a machine." To Confucius, the search for true manhood is a search for the ultimate itself.

The identity of true manhood and ultimacy is ignored both by Hu Shih and Buber. The central spirit of Confucianism is neither ethical nor supernatural but existential. Goodness, for example, has neither a theological meaning for Confucius nor a purely ethical connotation but an existential one. To Confucius, man is good not primarily because he does good things but fundamentally because he *is* good. Therefore, *jen* is no closer to humanism than it is to supernaturalism. Whoever sees Confucianism as a quest for religious reality will be unable to agree either with Hu Shih's humanistic interpretation of Confucianism or Buber's supernaturalistic interpretation of it.

Having dismissed Confucian culture as irrelevant to occidental man, Buber, however, maintains that from China:

> . . . there is still something that we can receive and actually from the standpoint of the progress of our history, of our experiences in this world hour. That is not, to be sure, something of the great structure of the Confucian culture; it is something revolutionary protestant, though basically, of course, ancient. I believe that we can receive from China in a living manner something of the Taoist teaching of "non-action," the teaching of Lao-tzu.[1]

Concentrating on Taoist teaching of the *tao* and *wu wei,* Buber tries to approach authentic existence. His full interpretation of them is found in the introduction to his translation of Chuang tzu. Buber sees this Chinese teaching as neither theological nor ethical, simply because the teaching

[1]Buber, "China and Us," pp. 189-190.

has no subject-matter except itself. In other words, the teaching is not the representation of a reality external to it. It teaches neither theism nor atheism. It is the self-proclamation of the One, according to Buber:

> The teaching is not peculiar in that it concerns itself with the inner or receives its measure and sanction from it. . . . What is peculiar to the teaching, rather, is that it is not concerned with the manifold and the individual but with the One, and that it therefore demands neither belief nor action, both of which are rooted in multiplicity and individuality. The teaching, in general, demands nothing; instead it simply proclaims itself.[1]

Along with his view of *tao* as not rooted in individuality, Buber also sees it almost non-dualistically as experienceable only by the individual in his individuality:

> . . . it must be pointed out that Tao generally means no explanation of the world; it implies that only the whole meaning of being rests in the unity of the genuine life, that it is just this unity which is grasped as the absolute.[2]

He defines authenthic man as a man of unity and thus a man of *tao*. Authentic man is neither the product of ethics nor of science. He is the man who finds the fulfillment of the teaching in his own life. The wholeness of existence is to be found in the unity of genuine life. In this unity, neither "I" nor "Thou" are necessary components. Unity or *tao* has no external or objective existence:

> In the teaching all opposites of the wholeness are elevated into the One as the seven colours of the spectrum fuse into white light.[3]

> The teaching has only *one* subject: the needful. It is realized in genuine life. From the standpoint of man, this realization means nothing other than unity. But that is not, as

[1]Buber, *Pointing the Way,* as translated by Maurice Friedman (New York: Harper & Brothers, 1957), p. 33.
[2]*Ibid.,* pp. 45-46.
[3]*Ibid.,* p. 34.

it might seem, an abstract conception, but the most concrete living.[1]

If one does not regard Tao as the necessary whose reality
is experienced in unified life but as something separate,
then one finds nothing to regard: 'Tao can have no existence.'[2]

Thus the reality of genuine life is something neither to be
developed in time nor to be placed in a fixed place. Genuine life to Buber has no "It." Instead a man of *tao* is directed towards nothing or concealment:

> Concealment is the history of Lao-tzu's speech. No matter
> how mythicized the Sermon of Benares and the Sermon on
> the Mount may be, that a great truth lies at the base of
> each myth is unmistakable. In Lao-tzu's life there is noth-
> ing corresponding. In his words, in his writings, one marks
> throughout that his utterances are not at all what we call
> speech, but only like the soughing of the sea out of its full-
> ness when it is swept by a light wind.[3]

Thus objectively, Taoism is much ado about nothing. It is
no-thing, aimless, useless, as Chuang-tzu frequently points
out:

> His age, which stood under the domination of the Confu-
> cian wisdom of the moral ordering of life according to duty
> and aim, called Chuang-tzu a good-for-nothing. In parable,
> such as that of the useless tree, he gave his answer to the
> age. Men do not know the use of the useless. What they
> call the aimless is the aim of the Tao.[4]

Although the man of *tao* aims at attaining nothing but
unity, such unity is not static but ever changing:

> 'No thing can beget Tao, and yet each thing has Tao in it-
> self and begets it ever anew.' That means each thing re-
> veals the Tao through the way of its existence, through its
> life; for Tao is unity in change, the unity that verifies itself

[1]*Ibid.,* p. 34.
[2]*Ibid.,* p. 46.
[3]*Ibid.,* p. 42.
[4]*Ibid.,* p. 44.

not only in the manifoldness of things but also in the successive moments in the life of each thing. The perfect revelation of Tao, therefore, is not the man who goes his way without alteration, but the man who combines the maximum of change with the purest unity.[1]

There are two types of life. The one is mere thoughtless living, using life up until its extinction; the other is the eternal change and its unity in spirit. He who does not allow himself to be consumed in his life, but incessantly renews himself and just through that affirms his self in change—which is not, indeed, a static being but just the way, Tao—he attains the eternal change and self-affirmation. For, here as always in the Tao-teaching, consciousness effects being, spirit effects reality.[2]

Tao, therefore, is unity in change. And the man of *tao* is flexible. However, this inner pliancy is derived not from the unity of the world nor from the divine but from the unity of man. The unity in change is in the unity of man. All unity apart from man's unity is either a by-product of man's unity or reflection of it:

Here, too, the perfected man, the unified one, is described as he who directly experiences Tao. He beholds the unity in the world. But that is not to be understood as if the world were a closed thing outside of him whose unity he penetrates. Rather the unity of the world is only the reflection of his unity; for the world is nothing alien, but one with the unified man, 'heaven and earth and I came together into existence, and I and all things are one.' But since the unity of the world only exists for the perfected man, it is, in truth, his unity that sets unity in the world.[3]

Thus the unity in the world comes into being only when man experiences the unity in himself. In the experience, in the authentic life, the two primal elements of nature, *yang* and *yin* are united:

As the Tao of things only becomes living and manifest

[1]*Ibid.*, p. 47.
[2]*Ibid.*, pp. 47-48.
[3]*Ibid.*, p. 48.

through their contact with other things, so the Tao of the world only becomes living and manifest through its unconscious contact with the conscious being of the unified man. This is expressed by Chuang-tzu through the statement that the perfected man reconciles and brings into accord the two primal elements of nature, the positive and the negative, yang and yin, which the primal unity of being tore asunder.[1]

Authentic existence, which thus unites these two elements is creative life, and the man of *tao* is a creator:

The perfected man is self-enclosed, secure, united out of Tao, unifying the world, a creator, 'God's companion': the companion of all-creating eternity. The perfected man possesses eternity. Only the perfected man possesses eternity. The spirit wanders through things until it blooms to eternity in the perfected man.[2]

The action of a perfected man or a man of *tao*, according to Buber, is not to be confused with all that we call action. In his interpretation of *wu-wei*, Buber puts it in opposition to man's goal-oriented activity, and thus he equates it with non-action or non-interference. Thus *wu-wei* is to Buber turning away from all ethical activity. Turning away from ethics is remaining within one's self:

We have begun to learn, namely, that success is of no consequence. We have begun to doubt the significance of historical success, i.e., the validity of the man who sets an end for himself, carries this end into effect, accumulates the necessary means of power and succeeds with these means of power, the typical modern Western man.[3]

And there we come into contact with something genuine and deeply Chinese, though not, to be sure, Confucian: with the teaching that genuine effecting is not interfering, not giving vent to power, but remaining within one's self.[4]

[1] *Ibid.*, p. 49.
[2] *Ibid.*, p. 50.
[3] Buber, "China and Us," p. 190.
[4] *Ibid.*, p. 190.

> . . . For violence, to Lao-tzu, is already in itself dead, life-
> less because it is Tao-less.[1]

Furthermore, ordinary love, righteousness or virtue as a part of human activity has nothing in common with that of the man of *tao*:

> What men call love of mankind and righteousness has noth-
> ing in common with the love of the perfected man. It is per-
> verted because it comes forward as an ought, as the subject
> of a command. But love cannot be commanded. Com-
> manded love works only evil and harm; it stands in contra-
> diction to the natural goodness of the human heart; it
> troubles its purity and disturbs its immediacy.[2]

> They rest upon a man's standing opposite the other men
> and then treating them 'lovingly' and 'justly.' But the love
> of the perfected man, for which each man can strive, rests
> upon unity with all things.[3]

In similar fashion, Buber distingushes ordinary knowledge and the knowledge possessed by the man of *tao*.
Chuang-tzu has pointed out the relativity of all that is ordinarily called knowledge. What is taken to be knowledge is
no-knowledge, simply because all beings are transitory,
changeable, limited, and relative:

> All this signified only one thing for Chuang-tzu: that what
> men call knowledge is no knowledge. In separation there is
> no knowledge. Only the undivided man knows; for only in
> him in whom there is no division is there no separation
> from the world, and only he who is not separated from the
> world can know it. Not in the dialectic of subject and ob-
> ject, but in the unity with the all is knowledge possible.
> Unity is knowledge.[4]

> This knowledge is not knowing but being. Because it pos-
> sesses things in its unity, it never stands over against them;
> and when it regards them, it regards them from the inside

---

[1] Buber, "The Teaching of the Tao," p. 39.
[2] *Ibid.,* p. 53.
[3] *Ibid.,* p. 53.
[4] *Ibid.,* p. 52.

out, each thing from itself outward; but not from its appearance, rather from the essence of this thing, from the
unity of this thing that it possesses in its own unity.[1]

Buber's interpretation of Taoist religious thought and
his evaluation of it comes as close as any to grasping its inwardness and to an appreciation of its non-dualistic character, but his thought is not wholly free of the entanglements
of opposites. And the later development of his thought has
been towards dualism as a condition of dialogue. To
Buber, Taoism is a mysticism that puts strong emphasis
upon unity. His conception of *tao* is misleading because
tao—as the Taoists see it—is not the unity which ignores
particular individuality. Although Buber speaks about *tao*
functioning in the changing world, he misses its cosmic intent. *Tao* is not merely the unity of a sage but life itself
which is limited neither to a few sages nor to ordinary
men. It is unlimited, infinite in the sense that life is not possessed or merely lived by a particular man or animate being. It is infinite because it belongs to neither the perfected
man nor to anybody. And yet it belongs to everybody.
Thus it is not to be objectified, not because it is possessed
or subjectified, but because it is all in all. From the beginning, it is not an unknown but it is the being of knower
and known. Therefore *tao* cannot be abstracted from itself
without being reduced to a corpse. *Tao* does not stand
over against man inviting him to a mystical union. With
tao there is no inside or outside and man's task is to realize *tao*. However, man's realization of it does not entail
any devaluation of individuality.

By the same token, *wu-wei* is not something which is opposed to activity. It is the realization of the original unity
of deed and doer. In this way, *wu-wei* is ontological rather
than ethical in connotation. It signifies a way of being
rather than a mode of behavior. The man of *wu-wei* does
not contradict himself with his own action. In him, nature

[1]*Ibid.*, p. 52.

does not stand in opposition to the human, and the divine is not set over against both the natural and the human. Thus *wu-wei* is neither passivity nor activity. It is a way of being one with all opposites. In other words, *wu-wei* is the non-duality of A and not-A, of *yin* and *yang*, of nature and man, of creator and creature.

The most widespread misinterpretation of Taoism, from which Buber himself is not wholly free, is that which regards it as teaching quietism, inactivity and the abandonment of striving. This equates *wu-wei* with one pole of the dichotomy of activity-passivity, and is tantamount to asserting that wholeness of life can emerge from opting for half of it. Though the partisans of salvation by grace and the champions of free will have each regarded salvation as emerging via the one means or the other, Taoism does not for its part proclaim one pole of a polarity as the indispensable means to non-duality. Non-duality is not a goal to be attained through the employment of this or that means, and deciding to cut down on activism is not practice of the *tao*. *Tao* or non-duality therefore is neither man's achievement nor given as grace. It is neither a unity which is made nor a unity which is given. Rather it is the root of all unity and all relationship.

Thus, *tao* is not ultimately different from *jen* which in Confucianism is the root of human relationships and Buber fails to see the ultimate concord of Confucius and Lao-tzu as it is experienced in Chinese religious culture, and his rejection of one and qualified approval of the other is blind to their mutuality.

In the end, Buber rejected both. In his foreword to *Pointing the Way* edited by M. Friedman, he says that his interpretation and evaluation of Taoism belong to a stage that he had to pass through before he could find his own so-called dialogical principle:

> In this selection of my essays from the years 1909 to 1954, I have, with *one* exception, included only those that, in the main, I can also stand behind today.

The one exception is 'The Teaching of the Tao,' the
treatise which introduced my 1909 translation of selected
Talks and Parables of Chuang-tzu. I have included this essay because, in connection with the development of my
thought, it seems to me too important to be withheld from
the reader in this collection. But I ask him while reading it
to bear in mind that this small work belongs to a stage that
I had to pass through before I could enter into an independent relationship with being. One may call it the 'mystical'
phase if one understands as mystic the belief in a unifica-
tion of the self with the all-self, attainable by man in levels
or intervals of his earthly life. Underlying this belief, when
it appears in its true form, is usually a genuine 'ecstatic' experience. But it is the experience of an exclusive and all-ab-
sorbing unity of his own self. This self is then so uniquely
manifest, and it appears then so uniquely existent, that the
individual loses the knowledge. 'This is my self, distinguished and separate from every other self.' He loses the
sure knowledge of the *principium individuationis,* and
understands this precious experience of his unity as the experience of *the* unity.[1]

Without entering into a discussion of Buber's later
thought, it may be suggested that it was not all progress
from the Taoist point of view but was a relapse into a dualism from which he had previously partly extricated himself. His more penetrating insights into Taoism do not
make sense if Taoism is only an egoistic experience mis-
takenly given cosmic significance. The authentic existence
of the Taoist sage as Buber had earlier eloquently described it can hardly come from the deluded confusion that
"this precious experience of his unity" is "the experience
of *the* unity." In other words, Buber now sees Taoism as a
psychological experience without ontological grounding;
the Taoist sage is only within himself; he has not attained
to the All. Buber is thus inclined to see the Taoist life as escape from the world and his own view as calling for a dialogue with the world. He does seem to have lost all touch
with his earlier appreciation of the oriental awareness that

[1]*Ibid.,* p. ix.

self and world are two abstractions. He now returns to the prejudice repeatedly encountered that the orient is committed to an infinite which denies the finite and in the light of this prejudice he chooses to stay with the finite. Taoist authenticity is now unreal; true authenticity lies in man's dialogue with the other:

> When this man returns into life in the world and with the world, he is naturally inclined from then on to regard everyday life as an obscuring of the true life. Instead of bringing into unity his whole existence as he lives it day by day, from the hours of blissful exaltation unto those of hardship and of sickness, instead of living this existence as unity, he constantly flees from it into the experience of unity, into the detached feeling of unity of being, elevated above life. But he thereby turns away from his existence as a man, the existence into which he has been set, through conception and birth, for life and death in this unique personal form. Now he no longer stands in the dual basic attitude that is destined to him as a man: carrying being in his person, wishing to complete it, and ever again going forth to meet worldly and above-worldly being over against him, wishing to be a helper to it. Rather in the 'lower' periods he regards everything as preparation for the 'higher.' But in these 'higher hours' he no longer knows anything over against him: the great dialogue between I and Thou is silent; nothing else exists than his self, which he experiences as the self. That is certainly an exalted form of being untrue, but it is still being untrue. Being true to the being in which and before which I am placed is the one thing that is needful.[1]

What had been considered as authenticity is no longer such. Now for Buber, the one thing needful is not mystical experience but dialogical humanism.

In his later period, there was still a third item in Chinese religious culture towards which he felt some sympathy, namely, Zen Buddhism, which he found markedly resembled Hasidism.

---

[1]*Ibid.*, pp. ix-x.

Buber sees Zen as a sect of later Buddhism. As a sect, Buber characterizes it as remaining quiet about absolute reality. Zen will neither affirm nor deny absolute reality:

> Zen (in Sanskrit dhyana, i.e., meditation) is the name of one of the varieties of later Buddhism, which laid hold of China in the sixth and Japan in the twelfth century. Its most important characteristic is that it declines to make any direct utterance on transcendent matters. According to tradition Buddha himself refused to speak of the realm of the Transcendent, and substantiated it by saying that such talk is of no avail in seeking the path of redemption. From this the Zen-school evolved the teaching, that man could not even think of the Absolute as such, let alone express it.[1]

Its refusal to speak about transcendence means for Buber that Zen is solely concerned with the immanent, that is, with worldly realities and worldly activities. This he takes to consist of man's ordinary life activity, and thus the Zen monastery is not a place to escape the world but a place for work. The intent of this community is neither transcendental nor contemplative nor speculative. It seems to consist of working, washing dishes, and doing something. In a nutshell, the gist of the Zen community is not just being there but doing something.

> Not by turning away from reality, but only by surrendering himself to it, can man achieve salvation. In accordance with this Zen cloisters are not places of contemplation for individuals, but fellowship settlements of landworkers; the work is the foundation of their life.[2]

> Through the activity of his whole spiritual-corporal being man achieves intimate intercourse with concrete reality, in intimate intercourse with concrete reality man becomes capable of grasping the truth, and in turn the comprehension of the truth leads to the highest concentration of deed.[3]

[1]Buber, *Hasidism* (New York: Philosophical Library, 1948), pp. 187-188.
[2]*Ibid.*, p. 189.
[3]*Ibid.*, pp. 189-190.

Zen Buddhism is thus not directed towards an abstract world but towards this concrete world of everyday reality. In the midst of man's world, man's intimate relation with reality is attained. Buber approves such Zen stories as the following:

> In the writings of Zen we find the theme in a narrower setting. A monk asks the Superior of his monastery, a great teacher of the ninth century, to reveal to him the secret of the doctrine. The teacher asks, "Have you had your breakfast?" "Yes," he answers. "Then wash the dishes," the teacher says to him. And as he hears this, the disciple receives the inner illumination.[1]

After quoting a similar saying from Hasidism, Buber claims:

> Both answers, the hasidic (sic) and the Zenic, are almost alike: the key to the truth is the next deed, and this key opens the door, if the deed is so done, that the meaning of the act finds its fulfillment here.[2]

Spiritual wisdom then is not to be found in formulations of abstract ideas but in human existence and active response:

> Hence truth in the world of men is not to be found contained in a piece of knowledge but only as human existence.[3]

> The teacher therefore is the man who does whatever he does adequately, and the core of his teaching is this that he allows the disciple to take part in his life and so grasp the secret of doing.[4]

> When a disciple, who is serving him, complains that he has not yet initiated him into the wisdom of the spirit, he answers, "From the day of your coming I have not ceased to instruct you in the wisdom of the spirit." "In what way, master?" asks the disciple, and the teacher explains to him, "When you brought me a cup of tea, did I not accept it? When you bowed before me, did I not respond to your

[1]*Ibid.*, pp. 190-191.
[2]*Ibid.*, p. 191.
[3]*Ibid.*, p. 192.
[4]*Ibid.*, p. 192.

greeting?" The disciple kept his head hanging, and now the teacher explains further, "If you want to see, look straight into the object; but if you try to brood over it, you have already missed it."[1]

Being concerned with the actual world and its everyday life, Zen is not knowledge about worldly reality and it is not known as an object:

> . . . one of the Zen teachers reproaches his disciples with this failing, that he "has too much Zen"; "If Zen is spoken about," he says, "I am filled with disgust."[2]

Thus, Zen is to Buber directed towards a truth which is unutterable. It is unspeakable, simply because it is so concrete and tangible:

> Hence the Absolute may not be apprehended through anything universal, instead it may be apprehended through the tangible and concrete, through something that we experience. Zen teachers tell the story of how Buddha, when he desired to impart the full teaching, held up a flower, and smiled in silence; only one in the assembled throng, his disciple Kashyapa, understood him and smiled too. The Zen-school traces its tradition back to Kashyapa, who received the mystery from Buddha. According to this the import of this tradition cannot be to hand down spiritual values in abstract speech. But also all established methods of meditation appear merely as more or less questionable expedients and not as the way to the attainment of truth; indeed some even designate them as a disease.[3]

Therefore, Zen truth—as Buber sees it—is set over against everything abstract and intangible. However, the tangible and the concrete are for Zen symbolic of a spiritual meaning beyond themselves. In other words, man's deed is somehow a means to attain Zen truth. The washing of dishes, for example, is understood as a symbol of spiritual activity:

[1] *Ibid.*, p. 192.
[2] *Ibid.*, p. 193.
[3] *Ibid.*, pp. 188-189.

In the Hasidic story the symbolic character of the occur-
rence is emphasized, whereas in the Zen story it remains
concealed, and in the literature the meaning of the saying
is discussed; it remains however almost without doubt, that
the washing of the dishes is here also a symbol of a spiritual activity.[1]

Buber's understanding of Zen appears to be a mixture of
insight and confusion. His insights are obscured and distorted because of his latent and continuing dualism. For
Zen the concrete is not favored above the abstract nor set
over against it. The abstract and the concrete are poles of
an opposition. What is truly concrete in the Zen sense is
life not thus dichotomized or polarized. Once the polarity
is present, there is a sin against the wholeness of life
whether one opts for concreteness or for abstractness:

After the establishment of this fundamental distinction, we
must consider afresh what seemed to us clearly to be common to Zen and Hasidism, the positive relationship to the
concrete. We have seen that in both the man in process of
learning and becoming was directed to things, to sensible
being, to activity in the world. But the motive force in
each is fundamentally different. In Zen the intensive direction towards the concrete serves to divert the spirit intent
on the perception of the transcendent from discursive
thought. The direction is, although aimed against the usual
dialectics, itself of a dialectic nature; it is not the things
themselves that are concerned here, but their unnotional
character as symbol of the Absolute, which is above all notion. Not so in Hasidism. Here the things themselves are
the object of religious concern, for they are the abode of
the holy sparks, which man shall raise up.[2]

The realism of Zen is dialectic, it means annulment; the
Hasidic realism is messianic, it means fulfilment. Just as,
linked with revelation, it heeds the past, so, linked with redemption, it heeds the future—both in contrast to Zen, for
which absolute reality is only accorded to the *moment*, as
this is the possibility of inner illumination, and before the

[1]*Ibid.*, p. 191.
[2]*Ibid.*, pp. 200-201.

moment the dimension of time disappears. Hasidism is, so far as I see, the only mysticism in which *time* is hallowed.[1]

All one can say is that for Zen there is no duality of the deed and its meaning. The deed is not a symbol of something beyond itself nor is it merely the limited thing it appears to be. It is not a physical vehicle or sign of a spiritual reality or meaning. What is it then? For Zen, the question can only be answered when it is truly asked. It cannot be answered in the course of a comparative study of Zen and Hasidism because in that context the question is not really confronted.

Buber quotes the famous Four Statements as definitive of the goal of Zen:

> Special transmission beyond the writings, no cleaving to words and letters, direct pointing at the soul of man, seeing into one's own nature, and the attainment of Buddhahood.[2]

Buddhism is not to attain a relationship between man and God, or man and things, or man and other men but to see into the individual's own nature. Since he interprets this to mean that the aim of Zen is to attain unity of man and himself, seeing into one's own nature is understood psychologically, and signifies an experiencing of one's self as against other's selves:

> . . . but the actual path to the Absolute is only seen in the relationship of the man to himself. The historical Buddha, who has become in the Mahayana a divine being coming down to earth, is here entirely pushed aside by this Buddhanature which dwells in all souls, and which every man is able to discover and to realise within himself.[3]

> In a book ascribed to the first patriarch of Zen, Bodhidharma, we read, "If you wish to seek the Buddha, look into your own nature; for this nature is the Buddha himself."[4]

[1]*Ibid.*, p. 201.
[2]*Ibid.*, p. 197.
[3]*Ibid.*, p. 197.
[4]*Ibid.*, p. 197.

The path towards the ultimacy lies in one's own self. Apart from seeing into one's own nature, all externalities including Buddha-doctrine and Buddha's image are idols. Here again Buber wholly misconstrues the substance of Zen. The path of the Absolute does not for Zen lie "in the relationship of the man to himself" but rather in the awakening to the true self. Zen is not a form of empirical introspection. It is not an experiencing of the psychological self. When Zen speaks of seeing into one's own nature, *one's own* is not a possession. It is not in contrast to what is not one's own. One's own means what one truly is, and this truth is not limited to a psychological self. What is truly one's own is that which is not caught in the dichotomy of self and other.

Buber's error here is one he shares with many others, and is generally to be found in the attempts of psychologists and psychiatrists to avail themselves of the content of Zen or to show that their methods of psychotherapy are essentially akin to Zen. Jung's approach to Zen was thus purely psychological and omitted its ontological core. In his foreword to Suzuki's *Introduction to Zen Buddhism,* Jung says about Zen's enlightenment as a psychological state of mind:

> The imagination itself is a psychic occurrence, and therefore, whether an enlightenment is called real or imaginary is quite immaterial. The man who has enlightenment, or alleges that he has it, thinks in any case that he is enlightened. . . . Even if he were to lie, his lie would be a spiritual fact.[1]

Fromm likewise sees Zen as a radical psychotherapy and the psychotherapist functioning essentially as a Zen Master. He interprets Zen Enlightenment to mean that the aim of Zen is to attain a psychological *experience* of wholeness through making conscious the unconsciousness, and thus it lacks the ontological aspect of Zen Enlightenment. The

[1]See D. T. Suzuki, *Introduction to Zen Buddhism* (London: Rider, 1949), p. 15.

aim of psychoanalysis, he says, is to make the unconscious conscious:

> *Making the unconscious conscious transforms the mere idea of the universality of man into the living experience of this universality; it is the experiential realization of humanism.*[1]

And he equates this with Zen as follows:

> I would prefer the formulation: being aware of his own reality, and of the reality of the world in its full depth and without veils. A little later Suzuki uses the same functional language when he states: "In fact, it (the unconscious) is, on the contrary, the most intimate thing to us and it is just because of this intimacy that it is difficult to take hold of, in the same way as the eye cannot see itself. *To become, therefore, conscious of the unconscious requires a special training on the part of consciousness.*" Here Suzuki chooses a formulation which would be exactly the one chosen from the psychoanalytic standpoint: the aim is to become conscious of the unconscious, and in order to achieve this aim a special training on the part of consciousness is necessary.[2]

More recently we find a similar psychological explanation of Zen enlightenment in Johnston's *Still Point*:

> In Zen the conscious mind is, to all appearances, brought to a standstill. The stream is halted; it is blocked; instead of entertaining pictures and images I endeavor to be *Mu* or "nothing." Or, alternatively, I smash the reasoning process with the illogical problem called the *koan*. And in this way, the conscious mind is either swept clean of all pictures, remaining in total darkness, or else it is rendered incapable of thinking. Viewing this situation a priori, one might say that such a mind, totally emptied, should lapse into unconsciousness; or one might suggest that voiding the mind might induce sleep. But a posteriori we know that neither of these things happens in Zen. Rather does a new type of mental concentration set in; and the mind begins to work vigorously at another level. I have called this think-

[1]Erich Fromm, D. T. Suzuki, and Richard De Martino, *Zen Buddhism and Psychoanalysis* (New York: Grove Press, 1963), p. 107.
[2]*Ibid.*, p. 131.

ing "vertical," as opposed to the ordinary "horizontal" thinking when images are flitting across the mind. Thinking vertically, the stream of images halted, the mind goes down, down, down. . . . In other words, the horizon of consciousness is extended, broadened, deepened; or, put in another way, the unconscious comes up.[1]

Being concerned with a psychological experience of enlightenment, Zen is to Buber indifferent to a relationship between man and man which should be based on humility. In this way, Buber rates Hasidism more highly, among other reasons because in Hasidism

> . . . humility is counted one of the chief virtues, whereas in Zen, it is not mentioned.[2]

As proof, Buber quotes a typical story from Zen. It is a story about a youth who visits a Zen Master from a distant land:

> The youth knocks, and is questioned about himself and his desires. "I am able," he says, "to contemplate the foundation of my existence, and I desire to receive instruction." The teacher opens the door, looks at the visitor, and closes it again in his face. After some time the youth returns, and the performance is repeated. The third time the visitor pushes inside, the teacher seizes him by the chest, and cries, "Speak." As the youth hesitates, he rebukes him, "You blockhead," and thrusts him out. The door turns on its hinge, and one foot of the disciple is caught in it and breaks. He cries out, and in that very moment he receives the inner illumination. Later he founded his own school.[3]

He follows with a typical story from Hasidism which is quite different from a Zen master's attitude towards his disciple. It is about one of the disciples of Rabbi Bunam of Pshysha, Rabbi Enoch, who tells how he longed for a whole year to enter his teacher's room and to talk with him.

[1]William Johnston, *The Still Point* (New York: Fordham University Press, 1970), pp. 45-46.
[2]Buber, *Hasidism,* p. 195.
[3]*Ibid.,* p. 194.

Buber tries to convey a kind of humility hidden in the story:

> Once as he walked around the field weeping, the desire came upon him with unusual strength, and compelled him to run at once to the Rabbi. The latter asked him, "Why are you weeping?" Enoch answered, "Am I not a creature in the world, am I not made with eyes and heart and all limbs, and yet I do not know, for what purpose I was created, and what good I am in the world." "Fool," said Rabbi Bunam, "I also go around thus. This evening you will eat with me."[1]

It is not clear on the basis of what evidence Buber infers that humility is not to be found in Zen. Had he met any Zen sages and found them arrogant? Or was it that he had not come across any Zen stories which illustrated humility? Here in any case are two Zen samples of humility:

> Many pupils were studying meditation under the Zen master Sengai. One of them used to arise at night, climb over the temple wall, and go to town on a pleasure jaunt.
>
> Sengai, inspecting the dormitory quarters, found this pupil missing one night and also discovered the high stool he had used to scale the wall. Sengai removed the stool and stood there in its place.
>
> When the wanderer returned, not knowing that Sengai was the stool, he put his feet on the master's head and jumped down into the grounds. Discovering what he had done, he was aghast.
>
> Sengai said: "It is very chilly in the early morning. Do be careful not to catch cold yourself."
>
> The pupil never went out at night again.[2]
>
> Kasan was asked to officiate at the funeral of a provincial lord.
>
> He had never met Lords and nobles before so he was nervous. When the ceremony started, Kasan sweated.

[1]*Ibid.*, p. 195.

[2]Paul Reps, (Compiled) *Zen Flesh, Zen Bones* (New York: Doubleday & Company, Inc., no year given), p. 78.

Afterwards, when he had returned, he gathered his pupils together. Kasan confessed that he was not yet qualified to be a teacher for he lacked the sameness of bearing in the world of fame that he possessed in the secluded temple. Then Kasan resigned and became the pupil of another master. Eight years later he returned to his former pupils, enlightened.[2]

Buber's evaluation of Zen, despite his evident sympathy for it, seems almost dictated by his pre-commitment and his determination to see Hasidism as mankind's supreme religious achievement. *Mutatis mutandis* the same estimate is to be made of Thomas Merton's relation to Zen. On the one hand, Merton can say:

Zen is then not Kerygma but realization, not revelation but consciousness, not news from the Father who sends His Son into this world, but awareness of the ontological ground of our own being here and now, right in the midst of the world.[3]

But taken literally, this would make Zen closer to ultimacy than his own Catholicism. Christianity is from this standpoint second-hand in comparison with Zen which is first-hand. If this is so, why does Merton persist in the derivative realities which Christianity proclaims rather than plunging into the source which, he says, Zen points to?

The fact is that in the end, both Buber and Merton see religion not as the search for truth or the search for one's cosmic reality, but as the identification with and the championing of a particular tradition. Although they see Zen in a positive way, they never dream of appropriating it. The oriental does not see his religiosity as commitment to a creed or tradition but as the way to himself which is simultaneously the way to truth. From this standpoint, there is no such thing as comparative religion any more than there is comparative truth or comparative selves. Comparative religion can only mean comparative formalities, for there can

[2]*Ibid.,* pp. 56-57.

[3]Thomas Merton, *Zen and the Birds of Appetite* (New York: A New Directions Book, 1968), p. 47.

never be such a thing as comparative realities. To the Chinese, the *san chiao,* although they are complete in themselves, are never in contradiction with each other. As we have pointed out, this unity or harmony is something which Judaism, Christianity and Islam have never had. All these Semitic religions are theologically in opposition to each other, each claiming that its own religion is supremely ultimate and according to the others at most an approximate truth. Each of them asserts its absoluteness by to some extent negating the others. And Buber as well as Merton and Johnston like so many others seem determined to contrast Zen and their own religions' tradition. In short, they judge or prejudge Zen in the light of philosophical or theological principles which they had before taking up the study of Zen religious thought. Thus they did not allow themselves, to use Buber's word, to have a real dialogue with Zen. Their discussion is polemical and apologetic rather than ultimately truth-oriented. To the Chinese consciousness, man's ultimate task is not to choose a religion but to undo the invisible walls between religions by finding a truth which is not confining because it is not finite. This truth is the truth of non-duality. And for China, the relation between Confucianism and Taoism or Taoism and Zen must be non-dualistic if each is really spiritually true. Thus it is non-duality which is to be realized as the religion of China. And so-called three *religions* of China all aim at attaining the *religion* of China which proclaims the harmony of Heaven, Earth and Man. Confucianism proposes to move towards it through *jen,* that is, the truth of human relationship, while Taoism proceeds via the truth of nature or earth. And Zen points to Heaven or *nirvana* or *sunyata.*

The goal, however, is not a possession of Chinese religions but truth itself, reality itself, being itself and ultimacy itself. In this sense, non-duality stops being nondual as soon as anyone claims it. Man's task, then, is not to champion the truth as expounded by a particular religion but to seek for his true self through whatever religious structure is most natural to him.

CONCLUSION

What I have tried to do in this dissertation was to put forth the hypothesis that the deepest intention of oriental religious culture is to reach the life of non-duality, to illumine the meaning of nonduality and of its many implications, and to show that at least a goodly number of recent appraisals of that culture appear to be based on an inadequate appreciation of the meaning of non-duality and of its place in oriental spirituality.

To fully apprehend the meaning of non-duality and of its implications, the inwardness of oriental spirituality must be penetrated. The meaning of non-duality cannot finally be acquired by an objective analysis or by hermeneutical procedures alone, but only by the existential encounter with nonduality as a living reality and with living teachers such as "sage," "master," or "guru." Oriental religion in its ultimate nature has always transmitted itself not fundamentally through words and documents but through the living experience. Words are not the ultimate reality sought, but at best point to that reality. And thus the seeker for reality must go beyond words to find reality in itself.

Our sampling of recent religious thinkers seems to indicate a persisting bent towards dualistic modes of thought which in various degrees limits their efforts either to assimilate or to criticize oriental religious culture. This culture is centrally committed to the enterprise of grasping life in its unfissured wholeness. It perceives reality as that which is without a second and never as one pole of any dualism. It will not be forced into choosing between God and the devil, creator and creature, man and nature, mind and body, reason and feeling, self and others, time and eternity, this world and the hereafter, ideal and real, abstract and concrete, etc., etc. Occidental thought, per contra, has been haunted by the hosts of dualism. Its response has been to choose one pole of each dichotomy or the other or to assert both paradoxically or to seek a golden mean. From the oriental point of view, none of these are ultimate solutions, and there is no solution so long as the duality is posited. A solution is not to be found within the framework of the duality. A solution must be a dissolution of the duality, or positively stated, an entry into cosmic life, that is, life in its wholeness before it is split between A and not-A. This is the fundamental meaning of the highest teaching of oriental religious culture: reality is non-duality.

We have not attempted to fully document the hypothesis that nonduality is in fact the ultimate intent of oriental thought. For our present purposes it sufficed to show that texts can be adduced as support of the hypothesis and that in the light of these texts at least such thinkers as we have examined have not been wholly successful in their attempts to grasp the religiosity of the orient. Our hypothesis would be strengthened by a study—which is outside the scope of this dissertation—relating the "highest" goal of oriental religiosity to its "lower" manifestations. To show that the "lower" is in fact a misapprehension of the "higher" or an accommodation for pedagogical purposes would lend additional credibility to the hypothesis that nonduality is in fact the key which enables one to see the whole of oriental religious culture in its truest and most comprehensive light, that is in its depth as well as in its breadth. Unless one finally ties together the higher and the lower or the depth and the breadth, one is left with another duality.

Only if the task were completed in this way would we not seem to be begging a crucial question. As it is, critics may argue that we have only pointed to the possibility that the quest for the life of non-duality is one perennial element in the four major religious cultures of Far Eastern

Asia, but that we have not substantiated our claim that the life of non-duality is the highest aim of the oriental religions and its ultimate essence. Beyond clarifying our necessarily limited intentions as far as this dissertation is concerned, all we can do at this point is to yet again call attention to the peculiar status of the hypothesis we are putting forth. Its ultimate validation must be existential, and it is not to be ruled out as a possibility by any variety of methodological dogmatism. All methodologists would do well to heed the words of Whitehead:

> Obscurantism is the refusal to speculate freely on the limitations of traditional methods. . . . The obscurantists of any generation are in the main the practitioners of the dominant methodology. To-day scientific methods are dominant and scientists are the obscurantists.[1]

Aristotle states somewhere in his *Ethics* that the good is that which the good man does. This means that the good is not in the first instance an objectivity apart from human life, but rather that it is the good man who is the criterion of the good, and not vice versa. The good which man seeks becomes an abstraction when it is separated from the living man of goodness. May we not derive a clue from this as to the proper integral methodology for the study of oriental religion which would be to absorb it from its most exemplary living specimens?

What might have been the subsequent source of occidental thought if Aristotle had pursued this approach and if he had taken a parallel course in his *Metaphysics* and had similarly stated that the real is what the real man is? This would have meant that being is not to be grasped abstractly but is only to be entered into existentially. In any event, the non-duality of seeker and sought is from our point of view the key to the inwardness of the orient. That one knows reality to the extent that he becomes reality, and that the task is not to formulate an objective and external criterion of reality, but to be real oneself—this is the per-

---

[1]A. N. Whitehead, *The Function of Reason* (Princeton, 1929), p. 34.

spective of non-duality. May it not be that in this day of the shaking of the foundations of traditional occidental culture, the readily discernible impact of the orient stems precisely from a widespread conscious or unconscious disaffection with abstract and dualistic modes of consciousness?

Take the world-wide phenomenon of recent years which is designated as "youth culture." One of its conspicuous features has been the interest it manifests in the religions of the East. Young occidental people today are everywhere probing oriental religious thought and in many cases attempting oriental religious disciplines. What has engendered this interest? Is it simply fascination with the exotic or is it perhaps symptomatic of a transformation in the depths of occidental consciousness? What is certain is that many young people are in search of truth, honesty, or real identity and it is precisely for this reason that they find themselves at odds with much of traditional occidental culture. In the orient the search for the true identity is not the abstract search for "What is man?" but the existential confrontation of the question "Who am I?" It is for this reason that it appeals to so many of the young who hope that the search for true selfhood will be perhaps a way of freedom from all forms of externality.

In any case the search for true identity cannot be said to have been the main thrust of occidental religious experience. There truth has been mainly viewed as some kind of yielding to the will of God. From the standpoint of reality as non-duality, however, integrity or authenticity of being is not attainable through obedience to the will of another nor through any conformity with the revelation or the Law nor by imitating the life of another. All forms of dualism between creator and creature yield only the separateness of man's actual existence from his ultimate existence. Apart from his own realization of the ultimate truth, no amount of belief or conformity can be religious in the ultimate sense of the word. In other words, theology based on self-forgetfulness can never yield reality or salvation, and that

is perhaps why theology pursued non-existentially as a speculative enterprise seems to be barren to so many today.

The interest in oriental religiosity is perhaps not uncon-
nected with the decline of this sort of religion in the occident. The Judaeo-Christian perspective is less and less the
center of man's life as it was in the Middle Ages. Phys-
ically speaking, the church is increasingly empty. And inwardly speaking, the mind—which once had been fortified
by a vision of total meaning now is bombarded from every
side by a multitude of theories whose main quality is their
rapid obsolescence. It has frequently been said that the central fact of modern history in the occident is the decline of
religion, but what is becoming daily more manifest is the re-
sulting sense of alienation of man from himself, from other
men, from nature, as well as from any transcendence.

The correlative emergence of secularism as a way of
life has elicited the call for dialogue between religion and
secularism and beyond that to proposals that religion fully
integrate itself into secular culture by becoming "religionless religion." We owe the phrase to D. Bonhoeffer, who
proclaims that both God and the church are dead. Unlike
Nietzsche, he proclaims it as a Christian. Today man is no
longer religious, and he cannot be interested in religion as
separated from daily life. In this religionless situation,
Bonhoeffer wanted to promote the dialogue of religion and
secular culture by bridging the traditionally unbridged gulf
between the sacred and the profane.

In Bonhoeffer, the pendulum has swung to the opposite
extreme from Barth. For Barth ultimacy is "wholly
other." God has nothing to learn from the secular order,
and the source of all truth is the transcendent word of God
and not the culture of man. Bonhoeffer represents one reaction to the collapse of this extreme transcendental dualism.
Only what is not clear is how Bonhoeffer can evade the
total surrender to humanism or secularism. In other
words, in his proposal for "religionless religion," the religionless is much clearer than the religion. He wants to
have both the secular and the religions held together in a

unity, but for occidental man secular and religious have been at odds for so long that the rejection of one has automatically meant the advocacy of the other. May we perhaps not say that Bonhoeffer was reaching in the right direction but was in the end the victim of his dualistic conditioning?

Tillich has also tried to deal with the crisis in religion and with the problem of theology of culture. He proposes a new conception of religion not as a specific establishment based on an individual founder but as a state of being grasped by an ultimate concern which qualifies all immediate concerns. Religion as ultimate concern constitutes an openness to all existences, and in this way, he sought to bridge the gulf between the ground of being and human existence and thus the gulf between the sacred and the profane. Nevertheless, his ultimate concern is still in contrast with immediate concern and thus is still not equatable with integral concern for the wholeness of human life. Tillich's proposal thus engenders another form of dualism, although it tries to overcome the gulf between the religious and the secular. Nor is it clear that he succeeded in uniting his own universalistic definition of religion with his particular allegiance to one, any more than he was able to synthesize the God beyond God with the God who spoke from Sinai. This is not to minimize the significance of his herculean effort to make religion relevant to an age of existential crisis.

What seems clear is that the occident is moving from religion as a dualistic relationship between the divine and the human towards various efforts at encountering the divine within the immediacy of experience. In one direction this has meant groping towards the secular; in another direction it has meant the revival of the enormous interest in mysticism. The mystical approach to religion—which has often been dealt with as heresy in occidental religious history—has recently become for many an alternative to traditional religion. The current interest in oriental mysticism is partly the result and partly the cause of the currently burgeoning preoccupation with mysticism in the occident. In its deepest meaning the mysticism is the outcome of the effort to break through the dualism between the seeker and the sought, that is between the individual and ultimate reality. The oriental sense of religion has always been mystical rather than formal, ecclesiastical, theological or establishmentarian.

Contemporary psychiatry and psychotherapy have also shown an openness to the influences of oriental perspectives. The works of Jung, Fromm, Maslow, and Horney and others cannot be overlooked in this matter. Increasingly modern life has forced the psychotherapist to confront the existential question, "How can man authenticate himself?" Thus the search for identity in psychotherapy has brought it to the search for an absolute or cosmic identity which is for our hypothesis the heart of oriental spirituality. If there is any criticism to be made of these psychological gropings, it is that they are still too psychological and insufficiently ontological, i.e., they endeavor to deal with man's self-alienation without considering his alienation from the ground of being. Another way of voicing this criticism is to say that while many psychotherapists evince sympathy for the objectives of oriental spirituality, admire its exemplars and are even enamoured of its methods, there are few who seem aware of the price of the product.

Contemporary philosophical thought is also characterized by tendencies of disaffection with traditional modes of philosophizing, and while some of these would be hostile to what the orient represents, others would be and in fact are very friendly. The movement called "Existentialism" for all its diversity is certainly an attempt to call philosophy back to life and away from the preoccupation with abstractions. Existentialism means in the end that thought must be expressive of *Existenz*; in other words it opposes the duality of thinker and thought. As Kierkegaard somewhere puts it—the truth is to be the truth; to know the truth is to be enmeshed in error. Existentialism seems to be a rebellion against traditional philosophies which are not concerned with concrete life itself. And thus Existentialism abhors ivory-towered thought. Existentialism asserts that no less important than the conceptualization of reality is the life of the individual philosopher. Lived life is existentially more important than life as understood and the existentialist would convert Cartesian dictum, "cogito ergo sum" into "sum ergo cogito." Existentialism is characterized by a concern for authentic existence which has been neglected by traditional philosophies which have dealt only with concepts.

Heidegger in his *Being and Time* shows that the whole history of occidental thought has been busily preoccupied with *das Seiende,* and has let *das Sein* fall into forgetfulness. To Heidegger, *das Seiende,* is object, while *das Sein* is the ontological possibility of the object. His philosophy, which is supposed to deal with *das Sein* is called fundamental ontology. It is fundamental ontology in the sense that it is distinguishable from traditional ontology. His ontology, unlike traditional ontology, is not a study of beings but a study of the being of beings without which beings are unable to exist. In other words, his ontology is not objective but existential. In this way Heidegger wants to throw new light on the non-duality of being and human existence. This non-duality of *das Sein* and *Dasein* as human existence is so basic to Heidegger that Being for him is hardly distinguishable from authentic human existence. And man's openness to Being itself is very close to what the orient has termed nonduality. According to William Barrett, it is reported that Heidegger is reading D. T. Suzuki's works and has said to a friend that if he understands Suzuki correctly, this is what he has been trying to say in all his writing.[1]

A fuller survey of the relation of oriental religiosity on contemporary culture would also have to consider its considerable impact on poetry, music, literature and architecture. This we cannot undertake to do here. Suffice it to note that from the standpoint of non-dualism, a work of

[1]As quoted in William Barrett, ed. *Zen Buddhism* (New York: Doubleday & Company, Inc., 1956), p. xi.

art is not a copy of an external objectivity, but essentially the actualization of true selfhood. Creativity is for the orient the graceful non-duality of form and matter, of the artist and his work. Art is for the orient self-expression, that is to say, Self-expression, and the greater the art, the deeper is the nonduality of self and Self.

The ultimate art is the art of life itself and if we are correct in our reading of the central message of oriental religiosity, life itself becomes art, that is creative or real, when it is the living actualization of non-duality. When self and Self are not in opposition then man is neither imposing himself on life nor being imposed on by life, but one with it. When self and Self confront each other in separation, then life and Life are divorced, and one either tries the hopeless task of absolutizing life or one seeks for Life and denies life.

The search for wholeness or holiness is the religious quest in its deepest meaning as we understand it, if our hypothesis has not distorted the fundamental meaning of oriental spirituality. If we are correct, oriental spirituality is essentially not finally an affair of the orient as such but for all men everywhere. However, no one can be fully persuaded of this through scholarship alone. For scholarship may suggest its truth, but only one's life can validate it.

BIBLIOGRAPHY

Books

Ahlstrom, Sydney. *The American Protestant Encounter with World Religions*. Beliot College, 1962.

Akhilananda, Swami. *Hindu Psychology, Its Meaning for the West*. New York: Harper & Bros., 1946.

.... *Hindu View of Christ*. New York: Philosophical Library Inc., 1949.

.... *Mental Health and Hindu Psychology*. London: Allen and Unwin, 1952.

Allen, E. L. *Christianity among the Religions*. Boston: Beacon Press, 1960.

Altizer, Thomas J. J. *Oriental Mysticism & Biblical Eschatology*. Philadelphia: Westminster Press, 1961.

.... *Mircea Eliade and the Dialectic of the Sacred*. Philadelphia: Westminster Press, 1963.

.... *The Descent into Hell*. Philadelphia: J. B. Lippincott Company, 1970.

Anesaki, Masaharu. *History of Japanese Religion*. Rutland, Vt.: C. E. Tuttle Company, 1963.

.... *Buddhist Ethics & Morality*, 1912.

Appasamy, A. J. *The Gospel and India's Heritage*. London: S. P. C. K., 1942.

Arnold, Sir E. *The Light of Asia*. New York: Boston Roberts, 1891.

Ashby, Philip H. *The Conflict of Religions*. New York: Charles Scribner's Sons, 1955.

.... *History and Future of Religious Thought*. Englewood Cliffs: Prentice-Hall, 1963.

Aurobindo, Sri. *The Life Divine*. 2 Vols. New York: E. P. Dutton & Co., 1953.

Babbit, Irving. *The Dhammapada*. New York: A New Direction Publishing Corp., 1965.

Barnett, Lionel D. *Hinduism*. London: A. Constable & Co., 1913.

Barrett, W. *Irrational Man*. New York: Doubleday Anchor, 1962.

.... *What is Existentialism?* New York: Grove Press, 1964.

Beal, S. (trans.) *Sacred Books of the East*. New York: The Colonial Press, 1900.

Blakney, R. B. *The Way of Life*. New York: The New Amercan Library, 1964.

Blofeld, John. *The Jewel in the Lotus*. London: Sidgwick & Jackson, 1948.

.... (trans.) *I Ching*. New York: Dutton, 1966.

Blyth, R. H. *Zen In English Literature and Oriental Classics*. New York: A Dutton Paperback, 1960.

Bodde, Derk. *China's Cultural Traditions*. New York: Holt, Rinehart & Winston, 1961.

Buber, Martin. *Hasidism*. New York: Philosophical Library, 1948.

.... *Pointing the Way*. Translated and edited by M. Friedman. New York: Harper, 1957.

.... *On Judaism*. New York: Schocken Books, 1967.

.... *A Believing Humanism*. New York: Simon & Schuster, 1967.

Burtt, E. A. (Ed.) *The Teachings of the Compassionate Buddha*. New York: The New American Library, 1958.

Carpenter, J. Estlin. *Buddhism and Christianity*. London: Hodder and Stoughton, 1923.

Carus, Paul. *The Gospel of Buddha*. Chicago: The Open Court, 1894.

.... *Chinese Thought*. Chicago: The Open Court Publishing Company, 1907.

Cave, Sidney. *An Introduction to the Study of Some Living Religions of the East*. London: Duckworth, 1952.

Chai, C. and Chai, W. *The Humanist Way in Ancient China*. Bantam, 1965.

Chalmers, Lord Robert. (ed.) *The Meaning of Life in Five Great Religions*. Philadelphia: Westminster Press, 1965.

Chan, W. T. *A Source Book in Chinese Philosophy*. Princeton:

Princeton University Press, 1963.

.... *Religious Trends in Modern China*. New York: Octagon Books, 1969.

Ch'en, Kenneth Kuan Sheng. *Buddhism*. New York: Barron's Educational Series, 1968.

Conze, Edward. *Buddhism: Its Essence and Development*. New York: Harper, 1959.

.... *Buddhist Texts through the Ages*. Oxford: Bruno Cassierer, 1954.

Coomaraswamy, Ananda K. *Buddha and the Gospel of Buddhism*. New York: Harper & Row, 1964.

.... *Hinduism and Buddhism*. New York: The Philosophical Library (no year given).

Creel, H. G. *Chinese Thought from Confucius to Mao Tse-tsung*. Chicago: University of Chicago Press, 1953.

Cuttat, Jacques-Albert. *The Encounter of Religions*. New York: Desclee Co., 1960.

Danielou, Alain. *Yoga*. New York: University Books, 1955.

Das, Bhagavan. *The Essential Unity of All Religions*. Bombay: Bharatiya Vidya Bhavan, 1960.

Dasgupta, S. N. *A History of Indian Philosophy*. New York: Cambridge University Press, Vol. 1 (1932) to Vol. IV, 1955.

Davids, T. W. Rhys. *The History & Literature of Buddhism*. Calcutta: Susil Gupta, 1952.

Dayal, Har. *The Bodhisattva Doctrine in Buddhist Sanskrit Literature*. London: Kegan Paul, 1932.

De Groot, J. J. M. *Sectarianism and Religious Persecution in China*. Taipei: Literature House Ltd., 1963.

Deussen, Paul. *Outline of the Vedanta System of Philosophy*. Cambridge: Harvard University Press, 1927.

.... *The Philosophy of the Upanishads*. New York: Dover Publications, 1966.

Devanandan, P. D. *The Concept of Maya*. London: Lutterworth Press, 1950.

Dumoulin, Heinrich, S. J. *The Development of Chinese Zen after the Sixth Patriarch in the Light of Mumonkan*. New York: First Zen Institute of America, 1953. Translated by Ruth Fuller Sasaki.

Edgerton, Franklin. *The Beginnings of Indian Philosophy*. Cambridge: Harvard University Press, 1965.

Farquhar, J. N. *The Crown of Hinduism*. New York: Oxford University Press, 1915.

al Faruqi, Isma'il Ragi A. *Christian Ethics*. Montreal: McGill University Press, 1967.

Forman, Henry James, et al. *Truth is One*. New York: Harper & Bros., 1954.

Fromm, Erich. *Psychoanalysis & Religion*. New Haven: Yale University Press, 1950.

Fung, Yu Lan. *A Short History of Chinese Philosophy*. New York: The Macmillan Company, 1948.

.... *The Spirit of Chinese Philosophy*. London: K. Paul, Trench, Trubner, 1947.

Giles, Lionel. (Trans.) *The Sayings of Lao-Tzu*. London: J. Murray, Butler & Tanner Ltd., 1959.

Goddard, Dwight. (ed.) *A Buddhist Bible*. Thetford, Vermont, 1938.

Graham, Don Aelred. *Zen Catholicism*. New York: Harcourt, Brace & World, Inc., 1963.

Hanayama, Shinsho. *The Way of Deliverance*. New York: Scribner, 1950.

Harrison, M. H. *Hindu Monism and Pluralism*. New York: Oxford University Press, 1932.

Heiler, Freidrich. *Prayer*. Translated and edited by Samuel McComb, London: Oxford University Press, 1932.

Heiman, Betty. *Indian and Western Philosophy*. London: Allen & Unwin, 1937.

.... *Facets of Indian Thought*. London: Allen & Unwin Ltd., 1964.

Hill, W. D. P. *The Bhagavadgita*. New York: Oxford University Press, 1928.

Hilliard, Fredrick. *Man in Eastern Religions*. London: Epworth Press, 1946.

.... *The Buddha, The Prophet, and The Christ*. London: G. Allen & Unwin, 1956.

Hiriyanna, M. *The Essentials of Indian Philosophy*. London: Allen & Unwin, 1959.

.... *Outlines of Indian Philosophy*. London: G. Allen & Unwin, Ltds., 1956.

Hocking, W. E. *Re-thinking Missions*. New York: Harper & Bros., 1932.

.... *Living Religions and A World Faith*. New York:

The Macmillan Co., 1940.

.... *The Coming World Civilization*. New York: Harper
& Brothers, 1956.

Houdous, Lewis, *et al. A Dictionary of Chinese Buddhist Terms*.
London: K. Paul, Trench, Trubner, 1937.

Hogg, A. G. *The Christian Message to the Hindu*. London: S.
C. M. Press, 1947.

Hughes, E. R. *et al. Religions In China*. New York: Hutch-
ison's University, 1950.

.... *Ta hsueh*. New York: E. P. Dutton, 1943.

Humphreys, Christmas. *A Popular Dictionary of Buddhism*. London:
Arco Publications, 1962.

.... *Zen comes West*. London: Allen & Unwin, 1960.

Hu Shih. *The Chinese Renaissance*. Chicago: The University of
Chicago Press, 1934.

Hu Shih and Lin Yu-tang. *China's own Critics*. New York: Paragon
Book Reprint Corp., 1969.

Huxley, Aldous. *The Doors of Perception*. New York: Harper
& Row, 1954.

.... *The Perennial Philosophy*. New York: Meridian
Books, The World Publishing Company, 1968.

Iino, Norimoto. *Zeal for Zen*. New York: Philosophical Library,
1967.

Immanuel, R. D. *The Influence of Hinduism on Indian Christians*.
India: Leonard Theological College, 1950.

Isherwood, Christopher. (ed.) *Vedanta for the Western World*. London: George Allen & Unwin, Ltd., 1948.

.... *Vedanta for Modern Man*. New York: Harper &
Bros., 1951.

Jaspers, Karl. *Socrates, Buddha, Confucius, Jesus*. Harcourt: Brace
and World, 1962.

Jennings, J. G. (ed. and trans.) *The Vendantic Buddhism of the
Buddha*. London: Oxford University Press, 1949.

Joad, C. E. M. *Counter Attack from the East*. London: George
Allen & Unwin Ltd., 1933.

Johnson, Samuel. *Oriental Religions*. Boston: Houghton, Mifflin
& Company, The Riverside Press, 1877.

Johnston, R. F. *Buddhist China*. London: J. Murray, 1913.

Johnston, William. *The Still Point*. New York: Fordham University Press, 1970.

Keith, Berriedal. *Buddhist Philosophy in India*. Oxford: Clarendon

Press, 1923.

Kim, Ha Tai. *Logic of Life*. Seoul: Chung Won Co., 1962.

King, Winston L. *In the Hope of Nibbana*. La Salle, Ill.: Open Court Publishing Co., 1964.

.... *Buddhism and Christianity*. Philadelphia: Westminster Press, mcmlxli.

Kitagawa, J. M. *The History of Religions*. Chicago: University of Chicago Press, 1959.

.... *Religions of the East*. Philadelphia: Westminster Press, 1960.

.... *Religions in Japanese History*. New York: Columbia University, 1966.

Kraemer, Hendrick. *The Christian Message to the Non-Christian World*. London: Edinburg House, 1938.

.... *The Christian Message in a Non-Christian World*. New York: Harper & Brothers, 1938.

.... *World Cultures and World Religion*. Philadelphia: Westminster Press, 1960.

Landon, Kenneth P. *South East Asia, Crossroads of Religions*. Chicago: University of Chicago Press, 1949.

Latourette, Kenneth Scott. *Introductory Buddhism*. New York: Friendship Press, 1956.

Legge, James. (Trans.) *The Texts of Taoism*. New York: Julian Press, 1959.

Leeuw, G. van der. *Religion in Essence and Manifestation*. Trans. by J. E. Turner, London: George Allen & Unwin, 1938.

Lin, Yutang. *From Pagan to Christian*. New York: Avon Book Division, 1959.

Lloyd, A. *Shinan and His Work*. Tokyo: Kyobunkwan, 1910.

Lotz, Johannes B. *Sein und Existenz*. Basel: Herder, 1965.

Lubac, Henri de. *Aspects of Buddhism*. Trans. by George Lamb, London: Sheed & Ward Ltd., 1953.

.... *Amida*. Paris, 1954.

Lyall, Leonard A. (trans.) *The Sayings of Confucius*. London: Longmans, Green & Co., 1935.

Macnicol, Nicol. *Indian Theism*. New York: Oxford University Press, 1915.

.... *The Living Religions of the Indian People*. London: Student Christian Movement, 1934.

.... *Is Christianity Unique?* London: Student Christian Movement, 1936.

Marty, M. E., *et al.* Ed. *New Theology.* New York: The Macmillan Co., 1964.

Macquarrie, John. *An Existentialist Theology.* New York: Harper Torchbooks, 1965.

Mainkar, T. G. *Mysticism in the Rgveda.* Bombay: Popular Book Depot, 1961.

Malefijt, Annemarie De Waal. *Religion and Culture.* New York: The Macmillan Co., 1968.

Maurer, Herrymon. *The Old Fellow.* New York: The John Day Co., 1943.

McGovern, W. M. *Introduction to Mahayana Buddhism.* London: Kegan Paul, 1922.

McKenzie, John. *Two Religions.* Boston: Beacon Press, 1952.

Merton, Thomas. *Chuang-Tzu.* New York: New Direction, 1965.

.... *Mystics and Zen Masters.* New York: Farrar, Straus & Giroux, 1967.

.... *Zen and the Birds of Appetite.* New York: New Directions, 1968.

Moore, C. A. *Philosophy—East and West.* Princeton: Princeton University Press, 1944.

.... .ed. *Essays in East-West Philosophy.* Honolulu: University of Hawaii Press, 1951.

Moore, G. F. *History of Religions.* New York: Charles Scribners, 1937.

Morgan, K. *The Religion of Hindus.* New York: Ronald Press, 1953.

.... *The Path of the Buddha.* New York: Ronald Press, 1956.

Mourant, John A. *Readings in the Philosophy of Religion.* New York: Thomas Y. Crowell Co., 1956.

Müller, Max. *Lecture on Buddhist Nihilism.*

Murti, T. R. V. *The Central Philosophy of Buddhism.* London: George Allen & Unwin Ltd., 1955.

Nakamura, Hajime. *Ways of Thinking of Eastern Peoples.* Honolulu: East-West Center Press, 1964.

Neill, Stephen. *Christian Faith and Other Faiths.* London: Oxford University Press, 1961.

Nikhilananda, S. *Ramakrishna: Prophet of New India.* New York: Harper & Bros., 1948.

.... *The Upanishads.* New York: Harper & Bros., Vol.

I, 1949; Vol. II, 1952.

.... *The Upanishads.* (Abridged Edition) New York: Harper & Row, 1963.

.... *Hinduism: Its Meaning for the Liberation of the Human Spirit.* New York: Harper, 1958.

Nivedita and Coomaraswamy. *Myths of the Hindus and Buddhists.* New York: Dover Publications, 1967.

Nishitani, Keiji. *Science and Zen in the Eastern Buddhist.* Vol. I, No. 1.

Northrop, F. S. C. *The Meeting of East and West.* New York: Macmillan, 1947.

Noss, John B. *Man's Religion.* London: The Macmillan Co., 1969.

Ohm, T. *Asia Looks at Western Christianity.* Herder, 1959.

Okakura, Kakasu. *The Ideal of the East.* New York: E. P. Dutton & Co., 1903.

Osborne, Arthur. *The Collected Works of Ramana Maharshi.* London: Rider & Co., 1959.

Otto, Rudolf. *The Idea of the Holy.* London: Oxford University Press, 1928.

.... *Indian Religion of Grace and Christianity.* New York: The Macmillan Co., 1930.

.... *Mysticism, East and West.* New York: The Macmillan Co., 1932.

Parrinder, Geoffrey. *Comparative Religion.* London: Allen & Unwin, 1962.

Pearson, Nathaniel. *Sri Aurobindo and the Soul Quest of Man.* London: George Allen & Unwin Ltd., 1952.

Perry, Edmund. *The Gospel in Dispute.* New York: Doubleday and Co., Inc., 1958.

Phillips, G. E. *The Religions of the World.* Wallington, Surrey, England: Religious Education Press, 1949.

Piet, J. H. *A Logical Presentation of the Saiva Siddhanta Philosophy.* Madras: Christian Literature Society, 1952.

Plopper, C. H. *Chinese Religion seen through the Proverb.* Nanking, China, 1935.

Prabhavananda, Swami. *The Upanishads: Breath of the Eternal.* Hollywood: Vedanda Press, 1947.

Pratt, J. B. *India and Its Faith.* Boston & New York: Houghton Mifflin Co., 1915.

.... *The Pilgrimage of Buddhism.* New York: The Macmillan Co., 1928.

P'u Sung-Ling. *Chinese Ghost and Love Stories.* New York: Pantheon, 1946.

Radhakrishnan, S. *The Vedanta according to Samkara and Ramanuja.* London: George Allen & Unwin Ltd., 1928.

.... *The Hindu View of Life.* New York: The Macmillan Co., 1931.

.... *The Bhagavadgita.* New York: Harper & Bros., 1948.

.... *The Principle Upanishads.* New York: Harper & Bros., 1948.

.... *East & West.* New York: Harper, 1956.

.... *Brahma Sūtra.* London: G. Allen & Unwin Ltd., 1960.

.... *East and West in Religion.* London: Allen & Unwin, 1967.

Radhakrishnan, S. and Muirhead, J. H., eds. *Contemporary Indian Philosophy.* New York: The Macmillan Co., 1936.

Reichelt, L. K. *Truth and Tradition in Chinese Buddhism.* New York: Paragon Book Reprint Corp., 1968.

Reischauer, E. O. and Fairbank, J. T. *History of East Asian Civilization.* 2 Vols. Houghton, 1966.

Renoir, T. *The Nature of Hinduism.* Walker, 1963.

Reps, Paul. *Zen Flesh, Zen Bones.* New York: Doubleday & Co., Inc., 1960.

Saunders, Kenneth. *Ideals of East and West.* New York: Macmillan, 1934.

Schopenhauer, Arthur. *The World as Will and Representation.* Trans. by E. F. J. Payne. Clinton: The Falcon's Wing Press, 1958 (Vol. I, II).

Schweitzer, Albert. *Christianity and the Religions of the World.* New York: Doubleday, 1923.

.... *Civilization & Ethics.* London: A & C. Black, Ltd., 1929.

.... *Indian Thought and Its Development.* Boston: The Beacon Press, 1956.

Sedananda, Swami. *Hindu Culture in Greater India.* Delhi: All India Arya Dharma Suwa Sariya, 1949.

Shibayama, Senkei. *The Six Oxherding Pictures.* Japan.

.... *On Zazen Wasan.* Kyoto, 1967.

Slater, Robert Lawson. *Paradox & Nirvana.* Chicago: The University of Chicago Press, 1951.

Smith, Huston. *The Religions of Man*. New York: Harper & Row, 1958.

Smith, Wilfred Cantwell. *The Meaning and End of Religion*. New York: The Macmillan Co., 1956.

.... *The Faith of Other Man*. New York: A Mentor Book, 1965.

Stcherbatsky, T. *The Concept of Buddhist Nirvana*. Leningrad, 1927.

.... *The Central Conception of Buddhism*. Calcutta, 1956.

.... *Buddhist Logic*. (2 Vols.) New York: Dover Publication, 1926.

Suzuki, Beatrice. *Mahayana Buddhism*. London: Allen & Unwin, 1959.

Suzuki, D. T. *Asvagosha's Discourse on the Awakening of Faith in the Mahayana*. Chicago: Open Court, 1900.

.... *Studies in the Lankavatarasutra*. London: Routledge, 1930.

.... *The Lankavatarasutra, A Mahayana Text*. London: Routledge, 1932.

.... *The Essentials of Zen Buddhism*. Edited by B. Phillips. New York: Dutton, 1962.

Takakusu, J. *The Essentials of Buddhist Philosophy*. Trans. by Chan, W. T. and Moore, C. A. The University of Hawaii Press, 1949.

Thomas,.E. J. *The Life of Buddha in Legend and History*. London: Kegan Paul, Trench, Trubner, 1927.

.... *The History of Buddhist Thought*. New York: Barnes & Noble, 1959.

Tillich, Paul. *Christianity and the Encounter of the World Religions*. New York: Columbia University Press, 1963.

Toynbee, Arnold. *A Study of History*. London: Oxford Press, 1947.

.... *An Historian's Approach to Religion*. Oxford University Press, 1956.

.... *Christianity among the Religions of the World*. New York: Charles Scribner's Sons, 1959.

Van der Leeuw, G. *Religion in Essence and Manifestation*. 2 Vols. Harper & Row, 1963.

Wach, Joachim. *Types of Religious Experiences, Christian and Non-Christian.* Chicago: The University of Chicago Press, 1951.

.... *The Comparative Study of Religions.* Columbia Paperback, 1969.

Warren, H. C. *Buddhism in Translations.* New York: Atheneum, 1963.

Watts, A. *The Spirit of Zen.* New York: E. P. Dutton & Co., Inc., 1936.

.... *Behold the Spirit.* New York: Pantheon, 1947.

.... *The Supreme Identity.* New York: Pantheon Books, 1950.

.... *The Wisdom of Insecurity.* New York: Pantheon, 1951.

.... *The Way of Zen.* New York: Pantheon, 1957.

.... *Beyond Theology.* New York: Pantheon Books, 1964.

Waley, A. *The Analects of Confucius.* New York: Random House Inc., 1938.

.... *Three Ways of Thought in Ancient China.* London: Allen & Unwin, 1946.

.... *The Way and Its Power.* London: G. Allen & Unwin, 1965.

Weber, Marx. *The Religion of India.* Glencoe, Ill.: Free Press, 1958.

Wei, Francis C. M. *The Spirit of Chinese Culture.* New York: Charles Scribner's Sons, 1947.

Welch, H. *The Practice of Chinese Buddhism (1900-1950).* Harvard University Press, 1967.

.... *The Buddhist Revival in China.* Harvard University, 1968.

Wing-tsit Chan, Isma'il al Faruqui, and Jospeh M. Kitagawa and P. T. Raju. (Comp.) *The Great Asian Religions.* London: The Macmillan Co., 1969.

Yang, C. K. *China's Religious Heritage.* New York: Abingdon Cokesbury Press, 1943.

.... *Religion in Chinese Society.* University of California, 1961.

Zaehner, D. C. *The Comparison of Religions.* Beacon Press, 1962.

Zimmer, Heinrich. *Philosophies of India*. Edited by Campbell, J. Pantheon Books, Inc., 1951.

Articles and Periodicals

Bellah, Robert N. "Confessions of a Former Establishment Fundamentalist," in *Council on the Study of Religion,* Vol. I, No. 3 (December, 1970).

Phillips, Bernard. "Reflection on Zen and Humanism," in *The Humanist,* Vol. xxviii, No. 6, (November-December, 1968).

Tibawi, A. L. "English-Speaking Orientalists" in *The Muslim World,* 1963.

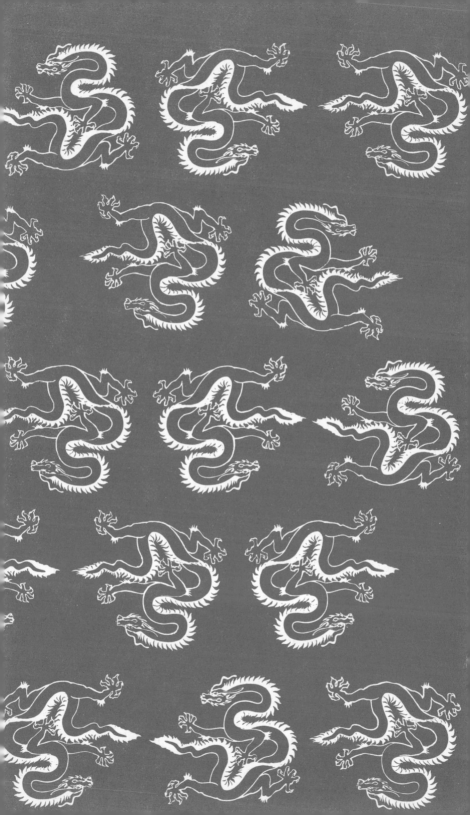

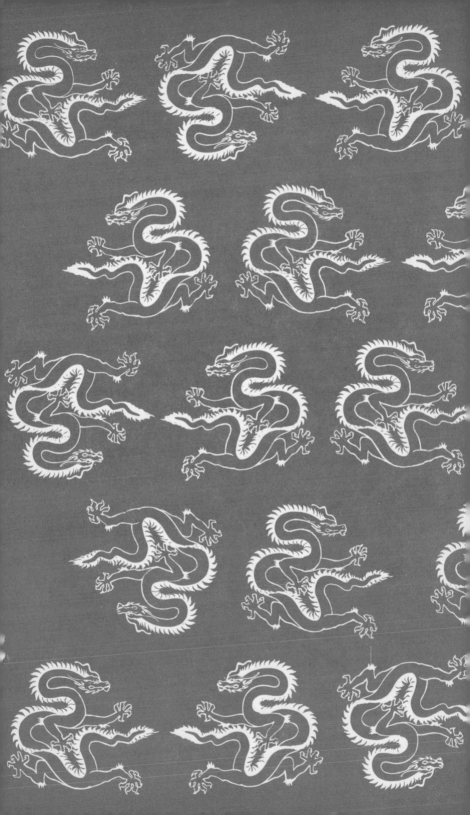